Opening
the
Hand
of
Thought

Opening
the
Hand
of
Thought

Foundations of Zen
Buddhist Practice

by

Kōshō

Uchiyama

Translated and Edited

by

Daitsu Tom Wright

Jisho Warner

Shohaku Okumura

Wisdom Publications
199 Elm Street
Somerville, MA 02144 USA
www.wisdomexperience.org

Library of Congress Cataloging-in-Publication Data
Uchiyama, Kōshō, 1912–1999
    Opening the hand of thought : foundations of Zen buddhist practice / by Kōshō Uchiyama ; translated and edited by Daitsu Tom Wright, Jisho Warner, Shohaku Okumura ; illustrations by Tai Hazard—Rev. and expanded ed.
    p. cm.
    Includes bibliographical references and index.
    ISBN 0-86171-357-5 (pbk. : alk. paper)
    1. Spiritual life—Sōtōshū. 2. Sōtōshū.—Doctrines. I. Wright, Thomas, 1944– II. Warner, Jisho Cary. III. Okumura, Shohaku, 1948– IV. Hazard, Tai. V. Title.
    BQ9438.U26 2004
    294.3'444—dc22
                    2004004435

23 22
9 8

ISBN 978-0-86171-357-8 ebook ISBN 978-0-86171-977-8

Cover design by Rick Snizik. Interior design by Potter Publishing. Set in Diacritical Garamond 10.5/18. Illustrations on pp. 78–79 by Kōshō Uchiyama. Additional illustrations by Tai Hazard.

Wisdom Publications' books are printed on acid-free paper and meet the guidelines for permanence and durability of the Committee for Production Guidelines for Book Longevity of the Council on Library Resources.

Printed in the United States of America.

Please visit fscus.org.

To all who are practicing
the buddhadharma

Sitting itself is the practice of the Buddha. Sitting itself is non-doing. It is nothing but the true form of the self. Apart from sitting, there is nothing to seek as the buddhadharma.

Eihei Dōgen Zenji

Shōbōgenzō—Zuimonki

("Sayings of Eihei Dōgen Zenji")

Contents

Prefaces

The Story of This Book and Its Author

by Jisho Warner

This is a very special book. Why does it deserve laurels, and your attention too? *Opening the Hand of Thought* goes directly to the heart of Zen practice. It describes the act of zazen—wholeheartedly sitting in the middle of your life—with great clarity and practicality. And it presents the wide, wide worldview that zazen opens up to you, showing how Zen Buddhism can be a deep and life-sustaining activity.

This book is a gift to us from one of the finest Zen masters, Kōshō Uchiyama Roshi. Though he never set foot outside Japan, his mind and heart flew across the Pacific, he sent his disciples here to teach, and he taught a great many Westerners at Antaiji temple in Kyoto, where he was abbot for ten years.

Antaiji was a very unusual place for its mix of monks and lay people practicing together and its mix of Japanese and Westerners. Even more remarkably, it was purely for practicing zazen and investigating the meaning of life. Most monastic centers in Japan are primarily training places for licensing as a temple priest, but Uchiyama Roshi felt it was most important to practice without any expectation of a reward. He said that practice at Antaiji had no bite, that people needed to just practice for the sake of practice. Those disciples who needed certification as temple priests he sent to regular monasteries for supplementary training.

Uchiyama Roshi's awareness of the West and his eagerness to make the Dharma and Zen practice available here, along with his background in Western philosophy and religion, meshed with his deep practice and understanding to create a unique voice. He lived by zazen, investigated with all his energy what it is to live a true life of Zen, and tells us about it in this book so we can delve into it for ourselves and verify the teachings for our own lives.

Zen is one long inquiry into how to live a truly full life. Life is universal, yet we feel separate from it and from each other. Taking what we need, discarding and preserving, enjoying and suffering, our life seems to be all about *us*. Uchiyama looks at what a person is, what a self is, how to develop a true self not separate from all things, one that can settle in peace in the midst of life. He dedicated his life to finding this out for himself and to passing it on to us, with great joy. Uchiyama Roshi's teachings came directly out of his life, from his youthful idealism to his early years of poverty when he learned to digest discouragement and turn despair into equanimity, and then to the wisdom of his old age. What is most important is that this major contribution to Zen teaching and practice is now available to you, for your own life.

"Opening the hand of thought" is the very act of zazen. It is the original Buddhist practice of not grasping and clinging, the practice of freedom, as it occurs in this very moment in your mind. As the subtitle says, this book offers you a foundation of understanding, intention, and aspiration based on actually doing Zen practice. There was an earlier *Opening the Hand of Thought*. It has been revised here and the language clarified. We have added new prefaces, an index, and extended end notes.

We three translators have all been transformed by Uchiyama Roshi's big mind. Shohaku Okumura was a young student when he met him. Okumura became his disciple and eventually settled in the United States to teach Zen. Daitsu Tom Wright went in the other direction, from Wisconsin to Kyoto, where he too became a disciple of Uchiyama Roshi. Wright stayed in Japan and was able to go on working with his teacher until Uchiyama's death in 1998. Jisho Warner first met Uchiyama's teachings in the United States as they began to take root here over twenty years ago. This book is a labor of love from Kōshō Uchiyama and from the three of us.

Teacher and Disciple

by Shohaku Okumura

In 1965 when I was a seventeen-year-old high school student, a friend of mine went to Antaiji in Kyoto and stayed there for a few weeks for a special summer practice period for students. In the fall my friend told me all about his experience there, sitting zazen, listening to the old priest's lectures and working with the young priest. He was particularly impressed by the way the young priest taught him how to make a fire, to keep the firewood burning well to heat water for the bath, and to extinguish the fire before the water became too hot. It was his first experience with a wood fire. He learned what being mindful and attentive means. The old priest was Kōdō Sawaki Roshi. The young priest was his disciple Kōshō Uchiyama.

In June of that year, Uchiyama Roshi had published his book *Self—Jiko*. I borrowed the book from my friend and became very interested in Uchiyama Roshi's way of life. The next February my friend had surgery to deal with stomach pain he had had since the previous fall. He was very sick for a few more months and then he died. After his death, his mother told me that he had had intestinal cancer and, because he was young, the cancer grew very quickly. This friend's death was one of the reasons I became a Buddhist priest. With his own death he showed me impermanence in actuality. He was a great teacher and bodhisattva for me.

I was very fortunate to encounter such a clear explanation of Zen practice in the very beginning of my practice. Even to a high school student like me, it was understandable. I began to see that our thoughts are the same as clouds. In our upright sitting all different kinds of thoughts come up, stay for a while, and disappear. We just let them come up and let them go away, not controlling our mind or preventing thoughts from coming up and passing away, not grasping or chasing after them either. We try to keep the same upright, immovable posture no matter what condition we are in, and to trust that above the clouds of thoughts, Buddha's wisdom and compassion are shining like the sun in a clear blue sky. This is what "opening the hand of thought" has come to mean in my life.

When I first read Uchiyama Roshi's book *Self—Jiko* in 1965, I wanted to become Uchiyama's disciple even though I knew nothing about Buddhism or Zen. After I graduated from high school, I tried to visit Antaiji, but it was a very small temple with no temple gate marking the entrance, so I could not find it. Fortunately, soon after I entered college, Uchiyama Roshi came to Tokyo to give a public talk about "being in your right mind between being insane and being brainless." His talk was very humorous and understandable even to me. I was sure he would become my teacher.

A few months later, I started to attend a zazen group at a small house in the graveyard of a big temple not far from the university. I attended my first five-day sesshin at Antaiji in January 1969. The sesshin was exactly as Uchiyama Roshi had described in his book. It was a very difficult experience for me since I was so inexperienced, the zendo at Antaiji was very cold, and I was sleepy all the time and in a lot of pain. When the sesshin was over, I was extremely happy and thought that it would be my last sesshin, but somehow I returned. Uchiyama Roshi sat facing the wall, the same as all the other practitioners. The small zendo of Antaiji was very full, and people sat two or three deep. I was impressed that there were several foreigners sitting together with the Japanese monks and lay practitioners.

The next spring I visited Antaiji again and asked Uchiyama Roshi to ordain me. He said, "I never encourage people to be ordained. It is very difficult to be a true monk. There are already many meaningless people wearing robes. If you want to be a true practitioner of zazen, I will accept you." I still appreciate his reply to my request—it left me no room for making excuses or shifting blame. Although I wanted to quit school and start to practice at Antaiji, he suggested that I finish school first, so I stayed at Antaiji for a few months and then went back to the university in Tokyo. I was ordained on December 8, 1970.

The day after my ordination ceremony, I had a chance to talk with him. He said, "Yesterday when I had tea with your father before the ceremony, he asked me to take care of you, but I can't do that. You should practice yourself and walk on your own legs."

That was the first teaching I received personally from my teacher. He said that he never faces his disciples: he faces the Buddha and walks in that direction as his own practice. And if I want to practice with him as his disciple, I should also face the Buddha and go in the same direction with my own feet. I appreciated what he told me and tried to rely on his teaching and not on him, practicing on my own and following his example.

After I graduated from Komazawa University I became a resident monk at Antaiji and I practiced there until February 1975 when Uchiyama Roshi retired. So, actually I practiced with him as a full-time practitioner at Antaiji under his guidance for only three years. It was not very long. But those three years were the decisive influence on my life.

When I graduated from the university and entered Antaiji, Uchiyama Roshi encouraged some of his disciples to study English and he paid our school fees himself. He had a vast perspective on the history of human spirituality, and he thought the twenty-first century would be an age of spirituality. He was also practical, and he thought the world needed people who had a thorough experience of zazen practice and could express the meaning of zazen in other languages. He encouraged his students to be pioneers instead of following fixed traditions, but he let us choose our direction for ourselves and never forced people to do anything. I was not particularly interested in studying English or practicing with people from overseas, but somehow I could not say no. This not-so-willing "yes" determined the rest of my life. Many Westerners became my friends, and practicing with them became natural to me.

After Uchiyama Roshi retired as abbot of Antaiji in 1975, I went to Massachusetts to practice with two of my Dharma brothers at Pioneer Valley Zendo. When I returned to Japan in 1981, Roshi encouraged me to begin working on translations with Daitsu Tom Wright, another of his disciples. Later I returned to the United States to try to continue what I learned from my master. I have the deepest gratitude for his teaching and practice, which always remained focused on the reality of life that includes all beings in the universe. Without his example I really would never have known how to live my own life.

On the Nature of Self

by Daitsu Tom Wright

One of the most challenging teachings of Buddhism and of Kōshō Uchiyama Roshi's teaching in particular centers around the nature of self and the meaning of the term *jiko*. "Self" is only a rough translation for *jiko*, though, because "self" has cultural, psychological, and philosophical meanings for English speakers that inevitably differ from the terrain the word *jiko* covers in Japanese. And even within Japanese, *jiko* has Buddhist meanings that differ from ordinary usage.

Jiko is defined in Nakamura Hajime's *Larger Dictionary of Buddhist Terms (Bukkyōgo Daijiten)* as both the individual self and "original self," which is the self that is born with or inherently has a buddha nature. All sentient beings possess the seed of awakened or awakening being, so original self is universal. Many Buddhist and Zen texts, like the *Blue Cliff Record,* have expressions like *jiko ichidan no daiji,* that is, clarifying "self" is of vital significance. A basic characteristic of existence that is of particular relevance here is that all phenomena (dharmas) are without an independent self. This is one of the three, or sometimes four, characteristics of existence that are a basic teaching of Buddhism and are discussed in this book. The translation of Buddhist terms as "self" leads to a big problem: if there is no self, then why is it necessary to clarify what the self is?

You may think it best to stick to English words, but if you do not know their origins it will be hard to make sense of the different meanings mixed together in the one seemingly simple word "self." What has traditionally been translated as "self" in the expression "all dharmas are without an independent self" is the Sanskrit word *atman*. In Japanese *atman* is translated as *ga,* a substantive, clinging, avaricious spirit or soul. This is not *jiko.* The first time I remember coming across the term *jiko* was when a senior monk at Antaiji pointed it out to me in the chapter entitled *Genjō Kōan* in Eihei Dōgen's *Shōbōgenzō.* At the time, I was reading through an English translation and was curious about what Japanese expression had been used. The passage turned out to be one of the most famous in the entire *Shōbōgenzō.* "To practice and learn about the Buddha Way is to practice and learn about *jiko.* To practice and learn about *jiko* means to forget *jiko.* Forgetting about *jiko,* one is affirmed by all things, all phenomena (all dharmas). To be affirmed by all things means to be made to let go of all concepts and artificial divisions of one's body and mind, as well as the body and mind of others, by those very things that affirm us."

It is not easy to understand the deeper layers of this passage without giving a great deal of thought to how the word "self" is being used. For example, in the opening line, where Dōgen equates the study and practice of the Buddha Way with the study and practice of *jiko, jiko* is being used in its broad, universal sense. In the next line, however, it is different. Although the line appears paradoxical, that learning about *jiko* is forgetting about *jiko*, what Dōgen is saying is that in learning about *jiko* in the broadest sense, that is, as our universal identity, we have to forget or let go of all the narrow ideas we might have about who we are.

To illustrate this point, Uchiyama Roshi used to bring up many concrete examples. On a crowded train, and in Japan that is a supremely concrete event, forgetting or not clinging to thoughts of who we are in terms of our status, age, or gender means to get up and give our seat to someone who looks much more tired than we are, without thinking about doing a good deed or being well thought of. The same spirit comes up in not clinging to a feeling of frustration when we have to cook for the group and won't be able to sit with everyone else. Or not getting upset because we have been asked to clean the toilet instead of our teacher's room, where no one will see what good work we are doing. The examples are limitless in all our lives.

As the years went by and Uchiyama Roshi asked either Shohaku Okumura or me how we were translating the term, he began to feel that perhaps it would be best not to translate it at all and just use the term *jiko,* allowing readers to taste it for themselves. For example, Dōgen coined the phrase *jin-issai-jiko.* The first character *jin* means complete or exhaustive, while *issai* denotes everything, all, or all-inclusive. *Jin* and *issai* are attached to *jiko* to make it more comprehensive. Setting these characters in front of *jiko*, we come up with something like complete-all-inclusive-self; accurate, but hardly a usable English expression. Kōdō Sawaki Roshi had an enigmatic expression *jiko ga jiko wo jiko suru,* where the word "self" is being used as the subject, the verb, and the object. It is almost untranslatable; perhaps "the self makes the self out of the self." Uchiyama Roshi had a similar expression, *jiko giri no jiko,* self that is wholly self. I believe Sawaki and Uchiyama coined their modern-day expressions as interpretations of Dōgen's *jin-issai-jiko.*

I have translated *jiko* as universal self or whole self, or more recently as universal identity. This is the same as *buddhata,* or awakened being, which I mentioned above. But this sounds quite abstract, when what we most need is to understand just what this means in the context of our daily lives. It is precisely this, Zen in our daily lives, that Uchiyama Roshi stressed more than anything else. After all, when asked to introduce ourselves or identify ourselves on meeting someone for the first time, we will most likely be thought weird if we reply, "Hi, I'm the Entire Universe, nice to meet you."

Jiko is used in everyday Japanese to identify ourselves in an individual sense, not as the universe. In modern Japanese *jiko* is used in terms like *jiko chushin,* or *jikoshugi,* meaning egocentrism or self-centeredness. In this case, the term is being used in a dualistic sense of oneself as opposed to another, and it implies a view of the individual that emphasizes our self-importance and degrades the importance of those around us.

Although he had studied philosophy, not psychology, at Waseda University, Uchiyama often referred jokingly to himself as a psychologist's psychologist. An endless parade of visitors came to see him—business executives from around the country, medical doctors, and psychologists, too. They came for counseling about the problems in their personal, self-centered lives, and he received them all. He also saw that some people's psychological difficulties might be alleviated by sitting in the zazen posture to get some composure. If doctors or psychologists felt their patients had greatly benefited from the incorporation of zazen into their therapies, all the better.

At the same time, he would point out to me that such uses of zazen should be understood as being examples of *bonpu zen*, that is, utilitarian Zen, or Zen for the sake of bettering or improving your condition or circumstances. If such Zen can be helpful to people, he never criticized its use, but he did point out that utilitarian Zen should not be equated with doing zazen without setting any preconditions or objectives. In other words, Roshi made a distinction between practicing zazen unconditionally, with an attitude of letting go of all thoughts of how zazen could benefit "me," and zazen done for utilitarian purposes. *Jiko* in Buddhism and in Dōgen's and Uchiyama's teachings is not about utility and self-improvement. Rather it has to do with seeing one's life from the broadest perspective and then functioning in a way that enables that perspective to manifest most fully through one's day-to-day activities.

The Theme of My Life

by Kōshō Uchiyama

The civilization that began in Greece, developed in post-Renaissance Europe, and has come to dominate the modern world is an intellectual civilization that defines and categorizes everything. But, having organized everything intellectually, the people under the strongest influence of this civilization seem to be on the verge of suffocating and have developed a great interest in the traditional Eastern world, where they hope to find an unlimited depth that transcends intellectual definitions. This search is fine, but people's ideas about "unlimited" and "transcendent" are likely to be confused.

Kyoto, the ancient capital of Japan and my home for many years, is over a thousand years old. Mountains surround it, and throughout the year mist and haze occur frequently. This mist envelops the mountains, where rocks and stones are heavily covered with moss. These moss-covered rocks and stones in the midst of silence seem to express unlimited depths. The mountains themselves, piled one on top of the other and wrapped in mist, contribute to an impression of mystical rapture. Innumerable books on Zen or the tea ceremony have featured pictures of Zen temples and teahouses with just such a background of moss-covered rocks and misty mountain scenes.

Of course, it's very fine that the mist makes the scenery around Kyoto so beautiful. But it would be a serious mistake to see in this kind of exotic landscape a key to Eastern thought, because when the hazy mists are cleared away by the true light of reason, there would be little left. The true depth of the East isn't a denial of human reason or a depth that must be hidden in an anti-intellectual fog. The unlimited of the East must still persist even after all the haze of confusion is cleared away by the light of reason. The depth of the unlimited is beyond the reach of any kind of reasoning, but it is not opposed to reason. It is like a sky without clouds or mist. The clear depth of the universe is the limitless truth discovered in the East.

What I want for you, the reader, is that you understand with your own intellect that Zen concerns the true depth of life that is beyond the reach of that intellect. This "life" is not Eastern or Western, it extends through all humanity. I hope that as you read you will look at your own life with a completely fresh mind and apply what I have written to your everyday life. That is the only place where the real world of Zen is.

I grew up in Japan during the Taishō era (1912–1926) and the first ten years of the Shōwa era (1926–1989). By the Western calendar, I was born in 1912. I graduated from college in 1935 and stayed on in graduate school for another two years. The earlier Meiji period (1868–1912) was an era that worshiped everything that came from the West. During the Taishō and early Shōwa periods, Japan began to appreciate its own historical roots. At the same time, the political scene saw a rise in ultra-nationalism, culminating in World War II. In other words, politicians took what should have been a natural pride felt by the Japanese people in their own cultural richness and manipulated it.

From the time I was in high school, I never took the slightest interest in nationalism. My eyes were always drawn toward a much larger world, and it has always been my dream to come up with some ideas that might be helpful to other people around the world. When I was a young child, I liked origami, or paper folding. I dreamed about coming up with a new idea for some origami figure that people anywhere could fold and enjoy.

My father worked on topographical models as part of his work, and he was an expert in origami. I suppose he first learned origami from his mother, just as I did; it was from my grandmother that my desire to create things through origami grew. By the time I was in college, my interest in creating new origami almost got out of hand. I invented a number of folds to make different shapes and created a style of making almost anything—flowers, animals, automobiles, buddhas—by folding just one square sheet of paper.

This was just an interest I had within the world of pastimes. Far more serious for me was my concern with the overall theme of my life. This came to be centered on the question of what the self is, and I wrote about this in a book entitled *Jiko*. This Japanese word *jiko* means "universal self" or "whole self." We live simultaneously as a personal self, an individual taken up with everyday affairs, and as a universal self that is inclusive of the entire universe. When I use the phrase "universal self" I mean it in the sense of a self that is living the whole truth of life. Trying to understand and live in terms of this reality has been the overarching theme of my life.

My father was curious about everything and threw all his energy into whatever aroused his interest, but there seemed to be no thread connecting all his activities. In contrast, my life has been dedicated to searching for a way that is connected and, moreover, is the most spiritually refined way for a person to live. What I've been pursuing is the most distilled way of living my life. I wrote a book titled *Jinsei ryōri no hon (How to Cook Your Life)* and in English originally titled *Refining Your Life* (since reissued under the title *From the Zen Kitchen to Enlightenment*). As I wrote in that book, what I mean by refining your life is aiming constantly at wholeheartedly living out the truth of life, not creating some pseudo-elegant lifestyle.

Underlying my life's theme are the deep connections Japan has with both Eastern cultures and Western traditions. First it was important for me to study and learn from the wisdom of the past. Then I needed to pursue my own individual lifestyle informed by this past. The first thing I did to realize this idea was to study Western philosophy and Christianity. By studying Western philosophy academically you can pretty much learn what it is all about, but Buddhism is another matter. It's virtually impossible to make much sense of it if you don't actually practice it. To investigate and understand Buddhism and zazen thoroughly, I became a monk. My becoming a monk was somewhat of a fabricated means for doing zazen, because it was easier to do zazen if I took on the lifestyle of a monk. It never occurred to me that I *had* to become a monk. When I was studying Catholicism, I had thought about becoming a novice priest just so I could study the religion, but regulations within the Church would never have allowed me to become one with that attitude.

I was ordained as a novice monk or priest on December 8, 1940. It was Pearl Harbor Day in Japan, across the dateline from the United States. I had been an intellectual, doing little besides reading and thinking, but I was determined to put all my energy into this practice. Later I wrote a poem I called "Poem for Leaving Home":

Like a sunbeam on a bright autumn morning,
I would like to become completely one,
Body and mind,
With transparent, wholehearted practice.

After the war I was extremely poor, like a great many Japanese people, and I had no home until I settled down at Antaiji, on the outskirts of Kyoto, in 1949. My early years at Antaiji were as hard as my homeless wandering years, but I continued my search for a true way of life. For me, understanding the universal self is inseparable from zazen, so in my book *Jiko* I talked a great deal about zazen. It was in this book that I first used the phrase "opening the hand of thought" *(omoi no tebanashi)*. It seems to me that zazen is the highest form of human culture.[1] Other developments have made human life both more comfortable and complicated, but not spiritually wiser.

I described two sides to a person who practices zazen. One side is the personal self that is always being pulled to and fro by thoughts about desires. The other is the self that is sitting in zazen letting go of such thoughts; this is an ordinary person living out universal self. The first side is like clouds, and the second is like the wide sky that the clouds float in. I wrote:

When we look up we tend to think that clouds mount up high in the sky, but I read that if we draw an eight-inch circle to represent the earth, the pencil line is the thickness of the entire atmosphere. The clouds are just things floating here and there, appearing and disappearing within that thin space.

Rain is just something happening under those miniscule clouds, but when rain keeps coming down, we think the entire sky is nothing but clouds and rain drops. In reality, above the atmosphere that is only as thick as a pencil line, there is always blue sky and the sun is shining. But we cannot even imagine that. How pitiful we living beings on the ground are!

In the same way, we are always covered with dark clouds of anxiety and sorrow, caught up in storms of anger and ambition, encounters with agony and despair. However, the clouds and rain of our thoughts are only happening within a pencil-thin atmosphere. This mental weather is simply happening within our thoughts that seek satisfaction. Outside of that sphere of thoughts, the sky is always blue, and the sun is always shining in it. When we can sit immovably like the encompassing sky, we can view and experience storms like pain and sorrow without being overwhelmed.

Zazen is precisely the posture of sitting in the sphere of absolute peace of mind that is like the big sky in which the many clouds of thoughts come and go. No matter how much zazen we do, poor people do not become wealthy, and poverty does not become something easy to endure. No matter how sincerely we practice, hardship is hardship. But simultaneously, we are in absolute comfort like the unperturbed sky and we do not need to think of our life in terms of difficulty and ease.

So here I am, having lived for over eighty years, and the thread that runs through all my life is my pursuit of living out the most refined way of life. In Buddhism this is referred to as the ultimate refuge.[2]

Walking the way of the universal self is what is called *butsudō,* the Buddha Way. This is the way I've been walking in my life. When people hear a phrase like *buddhadharma* or *Buddha Way,* they may get the idea of something very special or holy, but they are just expressions that have been passed down through the ages to orient us. What I've been trying to do in my life is to explain these things in a concrete way that might be understandable and helpful to anyone. I had to look at both Christianity and Buddhism and, intellectually, at Western philosophy, to realize both my own self-expression and my life vow of expressing the true meaning of living out the whole self.

I've always believed that the spirit to cultivate this life of self is very similar to the early American pioneer or frontier spirit. The difference is that those pioneers penetrated the western frontier in a spirit of staking private claim or possession to it. But this is not the attitude of one wishing to cultivate the frontier of the universal self.

What is most crucial is to remember to pursue the way of the self selflessly, not for any profit. Because we concretely are universal self, there is no particular value in talking about it. Yet if we don't make every effort to manifest it, just knowing about it is useless. To concretize the eternal, that is the task before us. Even if we have a cup of cool, clean water sitting right in front of us, if we don't actually drink it, it won't slake our thirst. The expression of universal self is a practice that is eternal, but to the extent that we don't walk it ourselves, it won't be realized, it won't be our path.

May this—the actualization of our universal self—be all our life work.

Just Bow

Putting my right and left hands together as one, I just bow.

Just bow to become one with Buddha and God.

Just bow to become one with everything I encounter.

Just bow to become one with all the myriad things.

Just bow as life becomes life.

This was Uchiyama Roshi's final poem, completed on the last day of his life.

Opening the Hand
of Thought

Practice and Persimmons

How Does a Persimmon Become Sweet?

The persimmon is a strange fruit. If you eat it before it is fully ripe, it tastes just awful. Its astringency makes your mouth pucker up. Actually, you can't eat it unripe; if you tried, you would just have to spit it out and throw the whole thing away. Buddhist practice is like this too: if you don't let it really ripen, it cannot nourish your life. That is why I hope that people will begin to practice and then continue until their practice is really ripe.

The persimmon has another characteristic that is very interesting, but to understand it, you have to know something about the Oriental persimmon. There are two types of persimmon trees, the sweet persimmon—*amagaki* in Japanese—and the bitter, mouth-puckering persimmon, called *shibugaki*. When you plant seeds from a sweet per-

1

simmon tree, all the saplings come up as astringent persimmon trees. Now, if I said that if you planted seeds from a sweet persimmon, all the saplings would become sweet persimmon trees, anyone could understand, but it doesn't seem to work that way. Without exception, all the saplings planted from sweet persimmon seeds are bitter. If you want to grow a sweet persimmon tree, what do you do? Well, first you have to cut a branch from a sweet persimmon tree, and then you graft it onto an astringent persimmon trunk. In time, the branch will bear sweet fruit.

I used to wonder how that first sweet persimmon tree came about. If the saplings from the seeds from a sweet persimmon all come up astringent, where did that first sweet persimmon come from? One day I had the opportunity to ask a botanist who specializes in fruit trees, and he told me this: First of all, the Oriental persimmon is an indigenous Japanese fruit; it goes back thousands of years. It takes many years to grow a sweet persimmon: even the fruit of a tree forty or fifty years old will be astringent. That means we're talking about a tree that's at least one hundred years old. Around that time, the first sweet branches on an astringent tree begin to ripen. Those branches are then cut off the tree and are grafted onto a younger astringent one. What took over one hundred years to grow on one tree is then transferred to another one to continue there.

In a way, Buddhism and our own lives are just like that. If you leave humanity as it is, it has an astringent quality no matter what country or what part of the world you look at. It just so happened, however, that several thousand years ago in India, in the culture of that day, a sweet persimmon was born; that was Buddhism. Or, more precisely, it was Shakyamuni Buddha who was born—like a branch on an astringent persimmon tree that after many, many years had finally borne sweet fruit. After a time, a branch was cut off that Indian tree and grafted onto the astringent rootstock that was the Chinese people of those days. From there, a branch bearing sweet fruit was brought to Japan and planted in that barbaric country. More recently, branches of those Asian trees have been grafted onto trees native to American soil.

Now, one thing about big old trees is that they wither easily. For the most part, there is not much Buddhism left in Asia today, except for Southeast Asia and some places in Central Asia, like Tibet. Japan is one of the few places you can find it, as withered and dried up as it may be. Now the sweet persimmon is being nurtured in America, and it needs to be tended and cultivated so it can flower and ripen in its new home. It doesn't happen without care and attention.

What I am saying also applies to your individual life. I would like for as many of you as possible to become sweet persimmon branches bearing the sweet fruit of a compassionate life, finding a true way to live as you settle on your astringent roots that are, after all, your own life, and your family, coworkers, and society.

I have had only one concern in my life: helping to discover and mark a true way of life for humanity. That is why I became a monk. Over the years I've never wished to become famous by the usual standards of fame. The only thing that matters to me is just to be an example of a true way of life that is possible for anyone anywhere in the world.

The Significance of Buddhist Practice

The starting point for Buddhist practice is how a person chooses to live out his or her life. Please don't misunderstand me when I use the words *Buddhist practice* or *Buddhism*. I'm not talking about some established religious organization. I'm concerned with how a person, any person, who is completely naked of any religious or philosophical clothes, can live out their life fruitfully.

Probably the vast majority of the four billion people in the world today live only in terms of pursuing material happiness. In thinking about their lives, most people devote almost all their energies to the pursuit of material happiness, or health, or prosperity. In contrast to that is the way of life in which we look to some Absolute to be the authority for our life, depending on a god or some idea to validate our way of life. A third approach is to search for some sort of permanent philosophical Truth—but so often what we find is something that has little or no connection to ourselves as individuals.

Now, in terms of these three ways of life, where does Buddhism fit in? Actually, it doesn't fit into any of them. To explain why, I'd like to return briefly to the story of my own youth. When I was in middle school, I never gave a thought to pursuing happiness materialistically; that always seemed meaningless to me. And the second lifestyle, that of setting up and obeying some sort of Supreme Authority, never appealed to me either. I could never get myself to believe in a great being and just follow along. That left the third alternative, searching after Truth. When I studied Western philosophy in college and graduate school, searching for a great truth, what struck me about this search was the way in which it was undertaken. The tradition of pursuing philosophical truth down through the Greek and German traditions required an extraordinary kind of passion. This kind of passion had no connection to your daily life, which had no value whatever with regard to Truth. It was supposed to be enough just to discover an abstract truth, but the daily reality of living that existed apart from and in contrast to philosophical truth continued to be a problem for me. So finally, although I learned a great deal from it, I could never get myself to throw my whole life into a philosophical pursuit of truth.

Pursuing truth was certainly the backdrop for the kind of life I wanted to live, but not truth in the sense of some sort of absolute, divorced from reality. In other words, when we talk about some ideal truth, or the way something should be in its ideal state, we can't help but feel a contradiction between that and the reality of what we are. My departure point was to move to the very edge of this contradiction and from there to find a truth that was undeniably real.

In the New Testament, Paul talks about the struggle between the form of what ought to be and the longing or voice of one's own body.[3] That is one area in which I always felt a connection with Christianity. Although I never came to believe in God in the Christian sense, I did feel strongly Paul's words concerning this struggle between body and spirit.

At that time in my life, I really didn't have a deep enough understanding to come out with a clear definition of truth in the philosophical sense. I didn't know what it was, but I was convinced that it was by truth or in truth that I wanted to live out my life. Gradually, a feeling grew inside me that the way I was searching for was very close to that talked about in the Buddhist teachings, and so I began to look more deeply into the Buddha Way. Finally, I became a monk. It is only after forty years of Buddhist practice that I finally feel I can begin to give a clear definition of truth.

The Four Seals

To begin with, there are two kinds of reality within our lives as human beings. One is the reality of chance or accident. The other is a reality having an absolute or undeniable nature. For example, perhaps I pour myself a cup of tea. I don't have to be pouring tea for myself, it's an accidental reality. There is no absolute reason why I have to be sitting here having tea, I just happen to be doing so. Seeing things in that way, most of our life consists of accidental realities: things could be taking place another way.

This is not to say there are no absolute realities. There are indeed some undeniable realities. For example, all living things die. There are no exceptions! No matter how much one is opposed to it or resists it, everything dies. This is an inescapable reality. So, unlike the accidental realities that just happen to come about, that could be changed by intention or design, there are undeniable realities that occur no matter how much we may resist them.

Any real or absolute truth must consist of living out our lives in accord with the inescapable realities that come about no matter how much we may oppose them. Buddhism as a religious teaching is founded precisely upon this kind of truth. During the period when trade between India and Greece and Rome was flourishing, around the time of Christ, when Mahayana Buddhism was developing, expressions and explanations concerning Shakyamuni's attitude and way of life became highly refined. Then, out of this, the true uniqueness of Buddhism developed. This uniqueness is embodied in the four seals, or principles, the *shihōin* (sometimes only the first three seals are mentioned, in which case they're known as the *sanbōin*). These four seals more or less summarize Buddhism.[4]

The first seal is that all phenomena are impermanent, *shogyō mujō*. The second is that everything is suffering, *sangai kaiku*. The third is *shohō muga,* sometimes glossed as all things and events (all *dharmas*) being without self. Maybe it would be clearer to say that things have no substantial independent existence of their own. The fourth seal is that nirvana is tranquillity, or quiescence, *nehan jakujō*. In Mahayana Buddhism, the expression *shohō jissō*—all things are themselves ultimate reality, or all things are as they are—is also used for this point, meaning that everything is truth in itself. These four succinct principles are unique to Buddhism.

Impermanence, *shogyō mujō,* means that every living thing dies. In other words, everything that has life loses life. Moreover, no one, least of all the living thing itself, knows exactly when its life will end. Life has a limit, and it is always in a state of uncertainty. This is the first undeniable reality.

I have mentioned that many people think that simply pursuing material happiness or riches is most important in life. But stand that way of life next to the reality of death and it completely falls apart. When a person who thinks he is happy because of his material situation has to face death, he's likely to fall into the depths of bitterness and despair. If happiness means having plenty of money and good health, then by that very definition, you're only going to hit rock bottom when it's your time to die. When you are faced with death, what good is being healthy or wealthy? That is why all of these materialistic pursuits only end in despair in the face of the undeniable reality of death.

What exactly is it that we have to learn from this first undeniable reality? We have to clarify what life and death really are. We have to know clearly just what it means to be alive and what it means to die.

In Pure Land Buddhism, there is an expression *goshō o negau;* that is, have hope for the next life. The belief is that life opens up after death. But that's not a very good understanding of the expression. What *goshō,* or "afterlife," refers to is the life that arises when one clarifies this matter of death. It means knowing clearly just what death is, and then really living out one's life. That is the most important thing we can learn from the first undeniable reality.

For us to remain unclear about life and death can only result in our dying in great despair and bitterness. This point leads to the second undeniable reality, that all things are suffering, or *sangai kaiku.* Suffering is not something that comes to attack me periodically; my whole life, as it is, is suffering. Nevertheless, I go around fighting with people, loving them, ignoring them, without ever being able to truly *see* that suffering. Actually, suffering in the deepest sense is all of that. In other words, as long as this matter of death remains unclear, everything in the world suffers. That is the meaning of the idea that all sentient beings are suffering. It is something that isn't talked about much simply because most people wouldn't have any idea of what it's about.[5]

I've mentioned that there are two types of realities, the one being accidental reality and the other being undeniable reality. When you think about it, I myself am just an accidental reality. After all, there is nothing that says I had to be born in twentieth-century Japan. I could just as well have been born in ancient Egypt, or Papua New Guinea, or indeed not have been born at all. In other words, being born in any age or in any place is a possibility, an accident, just as my being here right now is an accident.

From that we can say, then, that all the things I see in my world, and the world itself taking shape as I create it, are also an accident.[6]

For example, perhaps I look out the window and see that the weather has cleared up, so I think about what a nice day it is. But that is only because of where I happen to be. Somewhere else, it is surely raining right now. So, in a broader sense, it isn't quite right to say that "today" is a clear day. After all, somewhere there are people who are getting rained on or snowed on, and somewhere else, people must be laboring under a hot desert sun. Therefore, there's no reason to believe that only the things I see with my own eyes are absolutely or undeniably true.

There is no way we can say that our way of looking at things is absolute. If you and I are sitting together, you may think that we are both looking at the same cup in front of us, but it's not true. You look at it from your angle and from your perspective and I view it from mine. There's no ground for our saying that a fact we know or an idea we embrace is absolute.

Consider all the weather satellites circling the Earth. From their positions, the whole world looks like a map, and cities like New York or Tokyo look like some sort of mold growing on the surface. So it looks like people are just living in the same sort of mold that grows on a piece of old cheese. In that sense, I have no ground for saying that the world I see is everything; even weather satellites can show me that. If we look at a picture taken from the moon, the earth appears to be nothing more than a little ball with some sort of white fuzz floating around it. In brief, everything I happen to see is an accident.

Since my having been born in Japan in the twentieth century is just an accident, it follows that I—sitting here and looking out the window in this room of this particular house, at the moment when I write these words—am nothing but an accident. I'm only relative,

I'm not absolute. If I come to the conclusion that I am accidental, then naturally my thoughts are also accidental.

If both my mind and I are accidental, maybe the only thing remaining that could be called inevitable, or absolute, is God. That God must be absolute is the foundation for the rise of religions where only God can be true or real. Since we are nothing but things that have been created, we are just relative. The origin of this kind of religion thus begins with denial of oneself in favor of another, God.

The third way to approach life that I mentioned earlier says that because from an individual perspective everything is relative, or accidental, what should be relied on is abstract truth, or *logos*. This kind of truth is derived purely from human reason, or, in Greek, *nous*. This is the foundation of Western philosophy.

This kind of thought doesn't focus on the individual, but rather upon the whole of humanity. Though every member of humanity was born and dies, humanity as a whole doesn't die. Well, actually it will eventually—with the end of the Earth or before. But humanity has been around for over fifty thousand years and will probably be around for another fifty thousand. In other words, it wasn't born, in a certain sense, and won't die. The academic world does not take up the problem of things coming into being and dying. Rather, what it takes up is humankind as a phenomenon that was not born and won't die. However, to view things from that perspective entails coming to the realization that when I die I will be abandoned by truth.

How does Mahayana thought differ from these ways of looking at things? The Buddhist approach from a Mahayana perspective might be described this way: By accepting and properly understanding the true nature of both accidental and undeniable realities, and by living in accord with this understanding, the matter of living and dying will cease to be such a terrible problem.

The third undeniable reality is that all things lack substantial, independent existence; this is *shohō muga*. Since nothing is substantial by itself just as it is, there is nothing to hold on to. This means your thoughts are not something to hold on to either, so the only thing to do is to let go of all that comes into your head.

The expression "letting go of whatever arises" is my own way of expressing the idea of *kū,* or emptiness. This can also be interpreted as "without body or form," or not being tied to form. We can talk about this or that only because we grab on to or try to make some connection with something.[7] "Letting go of whatever arises" is not trying to forge a link with some outside object. This is the truth derived from the third undeniable reality.

The first undeniable reality is that every living thing dies, and the second undeniable reality is that we suffer throughout our lives because we don't understand death. The truth derived from these two points is the importance of clarifying the matter of birth and death. The third undeniable reality is that all of the thoughts and feelings that arise in my head simply arise haphazardly, by chance. And the conclusion we can derive from that is not to hold on to all that comes up in our head. That is what we are doing when we sit zazen.

What we call "I" or "ego" arises by chance or accident, so we just let go instead of grasping thoughts and "I." When we let go of all our notions about things, everything becomes really true. This is the fourth undeniable reality, complete tranquillity, or *nehan jakujō.* It is also described as "all things are as they are," *shohō jissō.* Therefore, when we let go of everything, we do not create artificial attachments and connections. Everything is as it is. Everything exists in one accidental way or another. This is the present reality of life. It is the reality of that which cannot be grasped, the reality about which nothing can be said. This very ungraspability is what is absolutely real about things.

Things being just as they are is also known as the *suchness* of things (*tathat>* in Sanskrit). But don't assume that what I've been calling "the present reality of life" is some fixed entity. It is not something that can be grasped or understood through reason or intellect. We let go, and that, as it is, is the reality of life outside of which there can be no other reality.

When we let go of our conceptions, there is no other possible reality than what is right now; in that sense, what is right now and here is absolute, it's undeniable. Not only that, this undeniable reality is at the same time the reality of life that is fundamentally connected to everything in the universe. This is undeniable reality. The truth to be derived from this is that right now is all-important.

Dwelling here and now in this reality, letting go of all the accidental things that arise in our minds, is what I mean by "opening the hand of thought."

When we think of "now" in the ordinary sense, we assume that there is a linear flow of time from the past into the present and forward into the future. Actually, it isn't that way at all. Actually, all that there really is, is *now*. As the scenery of the present, however, there is a past, present, and future. Let me say that again: *within the present*, there is a past, a present, and a future. The past and future are real and alive only in the present. This concept of time in Buddhist thought is very important. It is different from the notion in Western philosophy that time flows from the past, into the present, and on into a future in a linear way. According to Buddhist teachings it doesn't quite work that way. The past, present, and future are all contained within the present.

We have to realize that there is nothing outside of the present. Quite often people become shackled by the past. Believing that you came from a prominent family with a lot of money and feeling ashamed about your present condition is nothing more than being shackled to a conception of the past. Thinking that you have to repair a house because it appears to be old is only an idea; thinking that you have to fix it to preserve it unchanged is also just an idea. Likewise, to feel that you have to do something like become famous in the future is only to be shackled by your ambitious ideas about the future. What is most important is right now.

But again, within that "now" we have past experiences. Within the present, we have past experiences and a direction toward the future that we face. We have to vivify our past experiences and face toward the future—all within the present. Only if we master the realities of the past can they function vividly and smoothly in the present. Only if we have learned how to drive a car can we effectively use one to go somewhere. Doing exactly that is called *genjō kōan*, the koan of life becoming life. *Genjō* is the present becoming the present.

A man leaves his house after an argument with his wife, gets into his car all excited, and—bang!—he gets into an accident, all because he wasn't living fully in the present. This is a case of the present not completely living in the present. The truth to be derived from the Third Undeniable Reality is that we must give life to, or vivify, our past experiences and face the future, while living fully in the present.

Whether we realize it or not we are always living out life that is connected to everything in the universe. But when I say that,

I'm not talking about someone else's life, or life in general separate from myself. The life that runs through everything in the universe is me. I don't mean me as an ego, I mean my self in the true sense, the universal self. It is the foundation of all life experiences. Eihei Dōgen Zenji referred to the reality of life in this sense as *jinissai jiko,* or "the self that extends through everything in the universe." This self is not some fixed body, it's constantly changing. Every time we take a breath we're changing. Our consciousness is always changing, too. All the chemical and physical processes in our body are also constantly changing. And yet, everything temporarily takes a form. This is our true self, *jiko.* This is the real or universal self, or the reality of life, as I prefer to call it. Whatever way you put it, I am here only because my world is here. When I took my first breath, my world was born with me. When I die, my world dies with me. In other words, I wasn't born into a world that was already here before me, I do not live simply as one individual among millions of other individuals, and I do not leave everything behind to live on after me. People go through life thinking of themselves as members of a group or society. However, this isn't how we really live. Actually, I bring my own world into existence, live it out, and take it with me when I die.

I can't stress enough how essential it is to look very, very carefully at this universal self that runs through everything in the universe. You live together with your world. Only when you thoroughly understand this will everything in the world settle as the self pervading all things. As Buddhists, this is our vow or life direction. We vow to save all sentient beings so that this self may become even more itself. This is the direction we continuously face.

Shakyamuni Buddha said it this way: "All worlds are my world and all sentient beings—people, things, and situations—are my children." Dōgen Zenji's expression *rōshin,* nurturing mind or attitude, came out of this. My way of expressing this is "everything I encounter is my life"—*deau tokoro waga seimei.*

That is why our most fundamental attitude must be "just doing," or "doing nothing but this" *(shikan).* It's not a matter of thinking correctly about life. Thinking about life simply isn't enough. Our life is whatever we are encountering right now, and our practice is *shikantaza,* which is literally "just sitting." More broadly it means to put our energy into settling everything in our world here and now, where we really live.

Practice Is for Life

I want to take up the point of why it is so important to continue throughout our lives our practice of "everything I encounter is my life." The most essential point in carrying on our practice is to wake up this self that is inclusive of everything. This means we have to realize, over and over, that all sentient beings fall within the boundaries of our life.

For instance, imagine that you and I are sitting together talking. In talking to you, I'm not talking to some person who is other than myself. The face before me is reflected on the retinas of my eyes. You are within me. Facing you, I'm just facing myself. In other words, you exist within my universal self, and what I direct myself to is caring for the you that is not separate from me.

You should always bear in mind that all sentient beings are suffering. Everyone is fretting about something inside their head. For example, should I stay where I am or should I go somewhere else? That's the sort of thing we worry about, all too often. Actually, it doesn't matter where we are, since that is only a minor problem going on in our heads. There really is no such place as Japan. There really is no such place as America. Where you are living right now is all there is. For instance, if you were to have some idea that America really isn't a good place to practice and Japan is better, that would be nothing but a problem rumbling around in your head. When you look at things from the perspective of letting go of all your ideas and anxieties, what it comes down to is there is no America to leave or return to. To practice in Japan or in the States—either one is okay.

You might try looking at all the stuff that comes up in your head simply as secretions. All our thoughts and feelings are a kind of secretion. It is important for us to see that clearly. I've always got things coming up in my head, but if I tried to act on everything that came up, it would just wear me out. Haven't you ever had the experience of being up on a very high place and having an urge to jump? That urge to jump is just a secretion in your head. If you felt that you had to follow every urge that came into your head, well...

As far as human thought is concerned, anything is thinkable. But you have to have some stability, and think when all these things come up: Is this true or false? Is this best for me or not? You have to reflect upon yourself, and when you see yourself as relative, as accidental, you can't help but conclude that your thoughts must be accidents, too.

In bringing the buddhadharma to ripeness in your lives and in America, you have a big, big job. It is no simple matter to take the sweet persimmon of the dharma and transplant it in each of our lives so that all humanity may become a sweet persimmon tree instead of an astringent one. To do that you have to have a broad enough perspective to see that the frettings and grumblings that come up are all in your head and needn't be acted upon. You shouldn't use your own calculating mind to evaluate everything. Various things arise, but when you reflect deeply upon the accidental nature of yourself and your thoughts, you will no longer consider using them as the standard for your activities.

In order to truly see that using your thoughts as a standard is invalid, you simply have to practice. And to sustain your practice over time, it is invaluable to practice together with others, that is, in a sangha, a community. The *sangha* was originally the Buddhist monks and nuns living together, but now it has come to mean all those who practice the buddhadharma, particularly in groups. Practicing in a sangha is difficult; you have to actually taste the pain and suffering that you encounter there. Sometimes you want to go off on a tangent, or you want to quit the whole business, but you just have to keep plugging away.

After some time, though—and this takes years to really develop—you begin to get a perspective on things. You begin to realize that there's nothing more important than just letting go. Don't take what I've said to mean that problems won't come up anymore; they will. But you begin to see things for what they are: ideas, plans, and even how you perceive the things around you are just mental secretions.

Next, in practicing, and, if possible, being in a sangha, you mustn't forget vowing. By "vow" I mean that you must work and function toward settling everything around you. This should be your life posture as well as the foundation for all your activities. It is essential to live with the conviction that you are making history for the next generation. There isn't anyone else around who will do it. You have to realize this and plant your roots deeply. All most people see when they look at a large tree are the leaves and flowers, but it's the roots that you have to pay attention to. A tree won't develop fully unless the roots are buried deep. When the roots are in deep, then the tree will grow and beautiful flowers will blossom naturally.

It is also important to look carefully at our motives for doing zazen. As far as I can tell, it seems that far too many people who start doing zazen immediately begin to think about enlightenment, or satori. They get it into their heads that they have to attain enlightenment, and they sit just for that purpose. But they are way off base. To sit with the idea that you are going to gain enlightenment is just ridiculous. This is not too different from the way it looks from a Judeo-Christian perspective: In these traditions, only God is perfect; His creation is not. That is, no matter how great a person may become, it is nothing before God. Seeking satori is similar. Reality as it is is perfect, is enlightenment itself, but our small selves are certainly flawed. To think that people become great by doing zazen, or to think that you are going to *gain* satori, is to be sadly misled by your own illusion. Zazen is to Buddhism what prayer is to the Judeo-Christian traditions. Just as prayer is a giving up of our small petty desires and asking that God's will be done, zazen is also a giving up of our egotistical evaluations of ourselves (whether as superior or inferior) and entrusting our life to the power of zazen as embodied in the fourth seal, all things are as they are.

When you hear talk about ordinary human beings becoming great or gaining enlightenment, you can be sure it is not authentic practice and enlightenment they are talking about. In Christianity, people don't talk about human beings becoming great. When people start talking about how great their minister or priest is, God gets lost in the shuffle. How great a human being can become is negligible.

Fundamentally, no matter what kind of circumstances we may have fallen into, we are always in the midst of enlightenment. To the extent that we live in the world of letting go of all our own puny ideas, we live in the middle of enlightenment. As soon as we open the hand of thought and let go of our own insignificant ideas, we begin to see that this is so.

We are always living out the reality of life. However, as soon as we start thinking and calculating about things, we become, in a sense, suspended from reality. That is, human beings are capable of thinking about things that are not real. That is why I say that to realize the extent of our enlightenment is to see that proportionately we are not very enlightened. We have to be able to see that clearly. However much we become enlightened, it just is not very much. Our practice begins to ripen only as we start to be aware that although we live in the midst of enlightenment, the little we become aware of in life is just scratching the surface.[8] If we do not ripen at least that much, then we cannot really say we have been practicing zazen. Our practice will remain incomplete and astringent. But ultimately it does not have anything to do with a little or a lot. We just continue to practice, aiming to live a true way of life as best we can, neither worrying nor gauging what we are doing. In that environment the sweet persimmon branch will flourish naturally.

Opening
the
Hand
of
Thought
—
20

TWO

The Meaning of Zazen

Depending on Others Is Unstable

One day at Antaiji, I received a visit from a fifty-year-old American businessman who was the president of his own company. I speak only Japanese, but since he brought along an excellent interpreter, we had no trouble communicating. He said this to me:

"I have plenty of money and a wonderful family, but for some reason that I can't explain, about ten years ago I began to feel a terrible loneliness in my life. So I began studying Judaism, though I was unable to find any contentment in it. Then I studied Christianity, but I was unable to find any satisfaction there, either. Then, a few years ago, I heard a lecture on Zen Buddhism and began to feel that in Zen I might be able to find something that would satisfy me, and I've been studying Zen ever since. I've come to Japan to study

21

Zen more deeply, and I wonder what you think about this feeling of loneliness I have."

In reply to his very sincere statement and question, I said:

"Did it ever occur to you that this feeling of dissatisfaction or emptiness might be caused by your searching for the value, the basis, or recognition of your existence only in things outside yourself, such as in your property, or in work, or in your reputation? This empty feeling of yours probably comes up because you haven't yet found this basis within the reality of your own true self. In other words, you feel a hollowness in your life because you have always lived only in relation to other people and things, and haven't been living out your true self."[9]

My response seemed to fit his idea of himself exactly, and being moved by this, he immediately agreed with me. "It's just as you say. My day-to-day life seems to be filled with living in relation to things outside of myself. I'm sure this has to be why I feel such an emptiness inside. But...well, what should I do about it?" I replied: "You will never be able to resolve the uneasiness in your life by drifting around seeking things outside yourself. It is crucial to live out the truth of the self, which is self living the reality of universal self. Zazen puts this into actual practice. My late teacher Kōdō Sawaki Roshi used to say, 'Zazen is the self doing itself by itself.'"[10]

He nodded as if my words had been just what he had expected and went on, "That is exactly what I thought zazen was. I would very much like your permission to do zazen here at Antaiji."

My replies to his questions were not just my personal opinions. I merely told him what has been recorded in Buddhist sutras since ancient times. In the *Suttanipata,* one of the oldest Buddhist sutras, it is written, "To depend on others is to be unstable."[11] And in the equally old *Dhammapada* is the passage, "The foundation of the self is only the self."

This man was most unusual in his ability to accept these simple but very important passages with such humility and readiness. In most cases, much more explanation is necessary before a person can accept such ideas.

What is this thing we casually call "I"? It seems that this "I" stands out in relief only in opposition to or in encountering some "other."

For example, a man may see himself as something called a "husband" that exists in relation to his "wife" and a "parent" with respect to his "child." At work, he may feel that his identity as a "subordinate" is determined by his relation to his "superiors." Furthermore, he may regard himself as a "salesman" with respect to his "customers," a "competitor" with respect to others in the same line of business, a "poor man" with respect to a "rich one," unable to buy something he imagines as a good thing, a "loser" in contrast to a "winner," "powerless" in the face of society, and on and on, endlessly. It would be a wonder if a man whose awareness of himself was based on comparisons like these didn't become overwhelmed with feelings of inferiority. (See figure 1.)

If somehow he was able to avoid being crushed by an inferiority complex, it's easy to imagine him becoming consumed with striving after everything he perceives himself to lack. (See figure 2.)

Alternatively, a person with a lot of money or power might imagine she is superior to others around her, better and more important than everyone else. (See figure 3.)

FIGURE 2

The competitive self

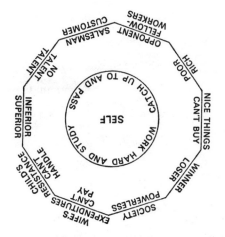

FIGURE 1

The inferior self

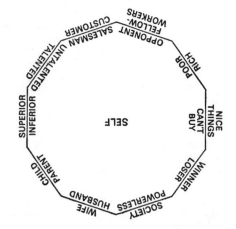

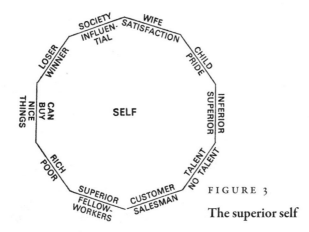

FIGURE 3

The superior self

In actuality all these people are in the same situation. They all conceive of "I" as something that is determined from the outside, as something defined in opposition to other people and things. Essentially, there isn't a bit of difference between them. There can be no doubt that ordinarily we live like this, being conscious of our "self" as something fixed from the outside and in opposition to others. Yet, if we think that only this is our "self," and if we live only by balancing this "self," comparing this "self" with other people and things, then I would have to say that we have lost sight of our self as the reality of life.

Jean-Jacques Rousseau wrote in *Emile* that every person, regardless of the wealth or status he may be heir to, is born naked and poor, and when he dies, must die naked and poor. This is certain, and yet, in between birth and death, people wear all sorts of clothes. One wears the splendid and gorgeous robes of a queen, while others spend their whole life wearing poor, tattered rags. Some people wear army uniforms; others, prison clothes; and others, monks' robes.

Of course our "clothes" aren't made only of cloth; there are also the clothes of class, status, fame, and wealth, all the clothes of our busy roles and cherished identities. There comes a time when we are stripped naked of all these things. There are also clothes called "handsome man" or "smart woman." Yet, no matter how beautiful a person is, there will eventually come the time when he or she must change clothes and don the dress of an "old person." Likewise, in the end, the genius may very well have to change into the clothes called senility. There are also the clothes of "superiority complex," "inferiority complex," "happiness," and "unhappiness," as well as those of belief, race, and nation. We change from one system of thought to the next, but when it is time to die, we have to take off even our clothes of racial distinction and die as completely naked selves.

Even though these are just outward trappings we wear in the interval between naked birth and naked death, almost all people are taken in by them. They assume that the entire problem of living is, out of all these possibilities, which nice clothes will they wear? I wonder if most people ever ask the question "What is the naked self?" While we are always undoubtedly living out some "self," usually we are not, in fact, living out the reality of our naked self, our true self. We concern ourselves only with the clothes we wear in our lives—that is, the self that is determined from outside and that lies in opposition to others. We seem to take it for granted that this is all there is to life, that "clothes make the man."

As long as this is so, it is not at all strange that people should find a hollowness in their lives. Whether they suffer from an inferiority complex, burn with a spirit of competition, or hold on to some idea of superiority, it is only natural that they all feel the same dull lack in their lives. To rely on others in order to know yourself is to be unstable. Of course this does not mean you should live in some kind of isolation from others. To be isolated is just as unnatural and unstable as to live always in reference to others. Your true self is beyond either relying on others or avoiding them in order to know who you are. We can't find true peace of mind until we live out the reality of the life of the self, since the foundation of the self is only the self. That is the universal self that I have been pursuing throughout my life.

The Self That Lives the Whole Truth

I have been using the word *jiko* as universal self for a long time. It is a very old Buddhist term, but I suspect it is quite difficult for people used to thinking in Western concepts to grasp. *Jiko* is used in modern Japanese in a variety of more-or-less psychological ways that can be summed up as "personal self." Most commonly, *jiko* is the conscious self—*ishikiteki jiko*. Next, people think of a self concerned with benefiting themselves as opposed to others, *rikoteki jiko,* or conditioned self. This is the self that arouses desires. Western psychologists would probably call this "ego."

In Buddhism, however, the term *jiko* refers neither to an egoistic self nor to a so-called conscious self. This is a major difference between the Buddhist term *jiko* and the psychological sense of self or ego. Buddhist *jiko* implies a self that goes beyond personal consciousness. However, when I start to talk of a self beyond consciousness, people immediately think it is some sort of mysticism. *Jiko* doesn't mean the individual psychological self, and it not something mystical. So what is it?

What we usually mean when we refer to our "self" is our conscious self, including what we are seeing and thinking right now, and our current role or identity. Actually, our conscious self is not only who we think we are right now, but also our ideas of who we think we have been in the past. In other words, the conscious self is the sum of our thoughts when we are awake from the time we were children up to the present. We take all those conscious thoughts and abstract them from our life and call that our self, but this is only part of the self.

Take for example sleep. No matter who they are, everyone sleeps, having opened what I call the hand of thought. When we sleep, everything does not cease to exist. Letting go of consciousness, our body continues to function; we breathe so many times a minute and our heart beats at a certain pace. The next morning we wake up and open our eyes; our thoughts start up again and begin to function. And again we put to work those thoughts of who we are that we held the day before. So what lives is not just who we are this morning; it includes the thoughts of who we are that we have had all our life until this morning.

I use the expression "opening the hand of thought" to explain as graphically as possible the connection between human beings and the process of thinking. I am using "thinking" in a broad sense, including emotions, preferences, and all sense perceptions, as well as conceptual thoughts. Thinking means to be grasping or holding on to something with our brain's conceptual "fist." But if we open this fist, if we don't conceive the thought, what is in our mental hand falls away. Our universal self, *jiko,* also includes that which lets go. Sleeping at night is a natural expression of your life with the hand of your thinking mind wide open. Nodding off while you are awake is something else entirely, from the perspective of the self. While you are awake, opening the hand of thought isn't dozing or thinking, it is the fine line between them where you really are right now.

The self of Western psychology is the Cartesian "I think, therefore I am." But actually, we are, whether we think so or not, and behind the conscious self your life continues even when you are unconscious or unaware. And precisely because of that we are alive with a life that includes our thinking self. In fact, it is because we have this actual ongoing life that the thought can occur that we are only our thoughts. So our true or whole self is not just an abstract self made of thoughts. Our whole self is the force or quality of life that enables conscious thought to arise, and it includes that personal, conscious self, but it also includes the force that functions beyond any conscious thought.

The whole or universal self is the force that functions to make the heart continue beating and the lungs continue breathing, and it is also the source of what is referred to as the subconscious.

This inclusive self is at heart the creative power of life. It is related to what the Judeo-Christian tradition calls the creative power of God. That power—what is immediately alive and also what is created—that is self too. If you want to use God as your referent, it is crucial to receive God as pure creative power, as being fresh and alive and working in and through yourself: no matter what I do or think, God is in all things and is working through me.

Whatever is alive—that is *jiko,* or universal self. All of this— thoughts and feelings, desires, the subconscious and the beating heart, the effort that enables other lives to function and the creative power of life itself—is what I mean by the "self." Saying "whole" or "true" or "universal" self is a way to try to include all the actual reality of life, and what I am saying here is that the actual reality of life is not something separate from the actual reality of your own life. Years ago I coined the expression *seimei no jitsubutsu,* "the actual reality of life." But the phrase was not very helpful because people would look at it and think about what it meant. They would put the reality I was pointing to outside of themselves. So I started using the word "self," and describing it in the utterly unphilosophical expression "self is what is there before you cook it up with thought."

> What comes before you boil it up
> Or fry it up by thinking,
> What precedes any processing by thought—
> The very quick of life, that is jiko.[12]

Since human thought continually cooks up everything, it is already removed from what is raw and fresh. Truly living out one's life, that is universal self, the self that is wholly itself. Concretely speaking, no matter how closely we might put our heads together, whatever it is we're looking at, we're going to see it differently. Your eyes see things with your vision and from your angle, that my eyes can never see, and vice versa. The world I see is solely mine. What I personally experience—life that is fresh and wholly my world, my perspective—that is also self, our personal or individual self.

The first-person "I" is totally my own life experience; it is separate from everyone else's. It is from that viewpoint that my teacher Sawaki Roshi pointed out that there is no way I can share even as much as a fart with another person. And yet, everyone living out their life as they experience it, as wholly theirs, is simultaneously the eternal, or universal aspect of self. The self is not universal in an abstract sense; it is so in a most concrete way. There is nothing abstract about all human beings living out one and the same fresh, original life force. There can't be anything more concrete than that.

Everything Is Just As It Is

Doing zazen is living out the reality of the life of the self, without assuming that "I" is determined by some relationship with other people and things. When we enter the world of Zen, we enter the world of practice where we live out the reality of life. Actually, this world of practice is nothing special, but it probably sounds unfamiliar.

Ordinarily, we live just as an "I" related to the world, an "I" that has only a social appearance and only a market valuation. In other words, we find the value of our existence only in the midst of others. We assume, on the one hand, that what is called "I" is an ordinary sort of thing, and on the other hand, that living a life of practice as our real "self" must be something special.

Western scholarship has turned its eyes away from the reality of life in yet a different way. Western thinkers, beginning with the early Greeks, have become used to grasping all existence solely by reason. This is grasping the meaning of things by establishing their precise relationship to other things, or grasping things in terms of definitions. Because of this approach, some Western philosophers try to grasp "self" and even the life force itself by definition. The life of the self does not come about by being defined. Life lives as real experience even if it is not understood or defined. Even the power to understand things by means of definitions is the power of our own life. This *ought* to be clear to us naturally, but all the Western rationalists' attempts at explanation leave it muddled. If one *thinks* about a reality that exists before the definitions of speculative thought, that in itself creates a kind of definition, recreating the problem. The speculated-about and redefined reality no longer exists prior to definition. You can easily wind up thinking that definitions are reality.

The foundation of Buddhism, with its origins in India, refers to the reality of life prior to all definitions. Different Buddhist scriptures express this same fundamental reality in various ways: emptiness of reality, reality as it truly is, beyond logos, inexpressible *tathata,* true emptiness.[13] Of course, since life produces all relative definitions, all definitions are life itself, but the reality of life cannot be bottled up in definitions of it. Although it produces all kinds of definitions, the reality of life transcends all definitions.

If we actually touch fire, we will certainly be burned, but if we merely say the word *fire* without actually touching it, we won't be burned. Likewise, if we only think of the word *fire,* our heads will not be set ablaze. Therefore, the *definition* of fire, whose nature is to burn all things, cannot itself be the *reality* of it. Fire exists apart from its definition. In Zen, it is said that a person knows cold things and hot things only when she herself experiences them.[14] Everything is taken in as the real life-experience of self.[15] This means there is no true value in definitions of things, reports of other people, or so-called pure observation of things, from which the life-experience of one's self is removed. As far as that goes, the difference I see between Zen and existentialism is that present-day existentialism is the philosophy of general existence, not the practice of the very life of the existentialist himself. The important thing for us is practice in which self truly lives out the life of the whole self, not discussions and observations of general existence.

From the standpoint of Western thought, where everything must be defined rationally, a reality that goes beyond definitions is nonsense and utterly impossible, but from the point of view of Zen practice, the very power that goes beyond just thinking and creating definitions with words must be the reality of life itself. D. T. Suzuki wrote about spirituality as what transcends or includes all dichotomies.[16] This world of spirituality opens up only when we actually practice the reality of life that transcends rationalism.

Is this reality of life that transcends definitions, language, and thought some mystical, esoteric world deeply hidden somewhere—something we are unable to talk about or even imagine? No, of course not, since in actuality we are always living out the reality of life.

If you put your hand up to your heart, you can feel it beating steadily. It does not beat because you are thinking about making it beat. Nor does it beat because of physiological or medical definitions. The hypothalamus regulates your heartbeat, for example, but it is not the cause of your heart's activity. As long as your heart is actually beating inside you, it is the reality of your life. A power beyond words and ideas is at work. It is this reality of your life, of your birth and death, not definitions of them, that I want to investigate here.

My breath is a little more under my control than my heartrate. I can take a few breaths by thinking about it, but it is completely impossible for me to be in constant conscious control of my breathing. It would be a terrible psychological problem to be afraid to go to sleep because I might forget to breathe so many times a minute during the night. I go to sleep entrusting my breathing to the great power of life beyond my control. Again, though this is not a power I control, since it is really working inside of me, it is nothing other than the reality of my life.

Let us go a little further with the concrete realities of our lives. I was born in Japan, and perhaps you were born in America or Europe. This is not something we chose by our so-called will, and yet, in fact, I am Japanese, and you are what you are. This is the reality of life that transcends our own measurement and discretion. Also, I am a Buddhist priest living a life of zazen practice in a certain temple in Kyoto, Japan. Is this way of life a way I chose by my own power? Yes, of course, in a certain sense, I did choose it. But where did I get the power to choose it? I cannot help but conclude that this choice, too, has been given life by a great power that transcends my own willpower and thought, whether you call it chance, fate, life itself, or the providence of God.

Using our intellect to come up with some answer to this we can only come up with a one-sided or abstract answer. Ultimately, all we can say is that the reality of life is as it is. The reality of the life of the self is simply to live life just as it is. Self does not exist because I think about it or because I don't think about it. Either way, this self, universal and personal, is my life. Zazen is a way of truly putting this reality of life into practice.

Living Out the Reality of Life

I have explained that the reality of life is the very living out of life just as it is, and that zazen is the practice of doing just that. But is there any other way to live besides living life as it is? Of course not. Whatever our way of life may be, that is the reality of life, so there is no possibility of living outside the reality of life. Nevertheless, it is all too possible to live losing sight of that reality, and because of that, to suffer and agonize about our lives.

One time a woman in her forties came to talk with me. She was distraught as she told me her story. She had always loved to paint and was quite talented. When she was in her twenties, her parents supported her and helped her make a life as an artist in Tokyo. Initially she met with considerable success. Her paintings were exhibited everywhere, often winning prizes, and even the critics gave her generous praise as an accomplished young artist. However, her brilliant beginning met with an obstacle. Just when her reputation was starting to grow, her father lost everything he had. It was still a little too risky for her to live only by her paintings, and she was also worried about her disappointed parents, so she returned to the country and did all she could to look after them. Years went by, and her parents grew quite old, but her unceasing passion for painting would not allow her to stay in the country and wither away, so she moved back to Tokyo, taking her aged parents along. She worked during the day and devoted herself to painting at night. She continued this effort for several years, but she was unable to win recognition the way she had in her twenties. Every painting she exhibited and placed her hopes in lost in competition. As a result, she was unable to sell any paintings and was forced to continue working to support herself and her parents, which sapped all her energy and spirit. Lamenting her unfortunate situation, she wept over being unable to develop her talent because her family had lost all its property.

While I totally sympathized with her inability to achieve her goal as a painter due to the setback in her circumstances, I rebuked her for her own sake:

"You're thinking about this all wrong. It's a big mistake to think that it is only natural for a person to receive a family inheritance. What is natural is that a person has no property at all. You were able to study painting by means of your family's wealth until you were past twenty. That's unusual, and something for which you should be grateful. Now, even though twenty-some years have passed, you're still lamenting your family's loss and being dragged around by fantasies of the past. You have to open your eyes to your present reality and start off with a totally naked self, possessing no property or anything else.

"Besides, you're still looking back to the time when you were in your twenties and the paintings you exhibited always won prizes for you, and wishing you could taste those days again. Isn't agonizing over things that don't work out just the way you want nothing but being dragged around by more fantasies? You have to begin with your present reality.

"What is most basic is that you paint because you enjoy painting, isn't that so? Can you let yourself be satisfied with that and with having a part-time job to support yourself? If you can make a living like that and enjoy painting the rest of the time, then you can have a rich life. This is something to be happy about whether you receive recognition or not.

"I haven't been doing zazen because I want to make it into something salable. I've been leading a life of zazen for thirty years, but in the first twenty, I was completely ignored by the world and practiced zazen in obscurity with barely enough to eat. But just by doing zazen, I was able to discover the meaning of my own life even in those circumstances. During the last ten years, people who are sympathetic with my attitude toward zazen have come to join me in sitting, but even now I haven't the slightest intention of making zazen into a salable product. I'm just doing my own zazen. For you, painting your pictures is your life. Shouldn't just that be your greatest joy?" She said she understood completely and went away with fresh vigor in her step.

We are always living out the reality of our own lives, although we very often lose sight of this reality, getting caught up in fantasies of the past or in our relationships with others. We end up being dragged around by those fantasies and by our comparisons of ourselves with others. Living like that, how can we not become filled with feelings of utter isolation and loneliness, overwhelmed by our jealousy and envy of those around us or by some other great suffering?

One time when I went to a place in the country, I could see from a distance a thick forest on the side of the mountain and I was able to make out the roof of a large temple hidden among the trees. I asked a local villager about it, and he told me that this temple used to be much larger, but it burned down and the present building was put up on a much smaller scale. Guided by the villager, I climbed up a long stone stairway. When I finally reached the top and had a look around, the temple, far from being small, was a magnificent structure that didn't seem to have been built at all recently. I began to wonder about what my guide had said, and I asked him just when the temple had burned down. He told me it had happened during the Kamakura period, in the thirteenth century! I burst out laughing, because his aggrieved tone of voice had implied that the temple had burned down recently, certainly during his lifetime. These villagers handed down to each successive generation a sense of personal loss about something that had happened hundreds of years before. Living near this handsome, imposing temple, they didn't really enjoy it because they were busy lamenting that it wasn't some other way.

On second thought, a thing that happened seven hundred years ago is undoubtedly a recent event for many people. Most religions encourage believers to "remember" events written in their holy books, events that may have happened thousands of years ago, and to act as if these things had happened to them personally. On the basis of these "memories" they wage wars and kill each other en masse. This is not limited to mythological and sectarian religions, either. It is exactly the same among all the many doctrines and ways of thought. Instead of looking at the fresh and vivid reality of life with their own eyes, people end up stifling that reality in the name of justice, or peace, or some fixed dogma.

All these memories and myths are produced by human life, so we cannot say they are meaningless. However, all these ideas and beliefs have only a conceptual existence that is fixed within our thoughts, they are not raw life-experience that is alive right now. We tend to plunge our heads too far into memories and fantasies, into religious dogma and rigid doctrines. When we admire them and believe in them blindly, becoming frenzied and fanatical, we become imprisoned by this fixed and conceptual existence.

We would be much better off if our past experience and wisdom were made to live within the raw life-experience of the self here and now. Instead we think that kind of conceptual existence is our real life of the present, and we end up being dragged around by our thoughts. We do things that only stifle raw life. This is happening all the time. When an individual is like this, he can be admitted to a mental institution as a schizophrenic, but when huge masses of people begin to act like that, there is no hospital big enough. Most unfortunately, such groups of fanatics eventually shape the very history of the human race. If we think about it, there is no doubt that everyone is always living out the reality of life. But so often we live blindly, so caught up in our thoughts that we think they alone are what is real and complete. This is a kind of insane reality. The important thing is to find a *sane* way to live out the reality of life. This is what a true spiritual practice is about: not spirit or mind separated from the body and the world, but a true way of life. This is what zazen is—a practice of living out the fresh reality of life.

THREE

The Reality
of Zazen

How to Do Zazen

The meaning of zazen must rest stably on the act of zazen itself, so the question of how to do zazen is essential. First of all, the room where you do zazen should be as quiet as possible. It should be neither too light nor too dark, and it should be warm in the winter and cool in the summer. Care should be taken not to allow wind or smoke in the room, while the room itself should be kept neat and clean. In other words, try to create a settled and peaceful environment where you can continue to sit on a regular basis. If possible, it is also good to enshrine a buddha statue, offer flowers, and burn incense. A buddha statue represents the tranquillity of zazen and is an artistic expression of the compassion and wisdom of zazen. This way, we create an atmosphere that supports our doing zazen. We should always take good care of the environment that supports our zazen, paying respect to the place where we sit, and bowing when entering the zendo, or sitting hall.

To complete your arrangements, lay down a large flat cushion, a *zabuton* or *zaniku.* On top of that, place a *zafu,* a round, firm cushion. Sit down on the zafu, facing a wall, and fold your legs. Sit on the front part of the zafu, not squarely on the middle of it. A few people can cross both legs by putting the right foot on the left thigh and the left foot on the right thigh in the very stable, classic full-lotus posture (see figure 4), but it is not possible for most people. You may be able to place your left foot on your right thigh (or your right foot on your left leg). This is called the half-lotus posture (see figure 5). Your knees should be resting firmly on the zabuton. This way, the weight of the upper part of the body can be distributed stably on three points—both knees on the zabuton and the buttocks on the zafu.

If you cannot place one foot on the other leg, you can sit cross-legged with both legs and feet resting on the zabuton, in the posture known as Burmese (see figure 6). If your hips or knees do not permit sitting cross-legged, you can sit in a kneeling position, known as *seiza,* and rest your buttocks on a low bench or on a zafu set on end (see figure 7). You can also do zazen sitting in a chair. This is more difficult, because it is harder to settle into a stable upright posture on a chair. Sit with your knees slightly lower than your hips, your feet planted on the floor, or on a cushion if necessary. You may find it helpful to use a cushion for lower back support, but the upper back should sit freely upright if at all possible (see figure 8).

Straighten your back, with your buttocks naturally but firmly pushing outward and your pelvis slightly tipped forward. Sit upright, leaning neither sideways nor front or back. Your ears should be in line with your shoulders, and your nose should line up with your navel. Keep your neck straight and pull in your chin. Close your mouth and put your tongue firmly against the upper palate. Project the top of your head as if it were going to pierce the ceiling. Relax your shoulders. Rest your hands at the crease of your torso and thighs, with your right hand palm-up in your lap and your left hand in the palm of the right. Your thumbs should touch lightly just above

FIGURE 4

Full-lotus posture

FIGURE 5

Half-lotus posture

FIGURE 6

Burmese posture

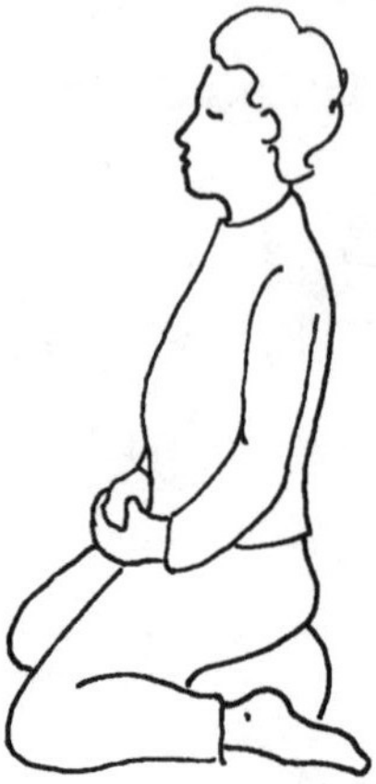

FIGURE 7

Kneeling posture

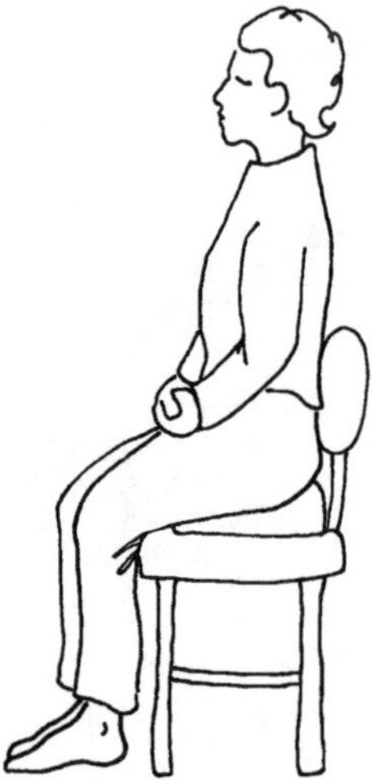

FIGURE 8

Chair posture

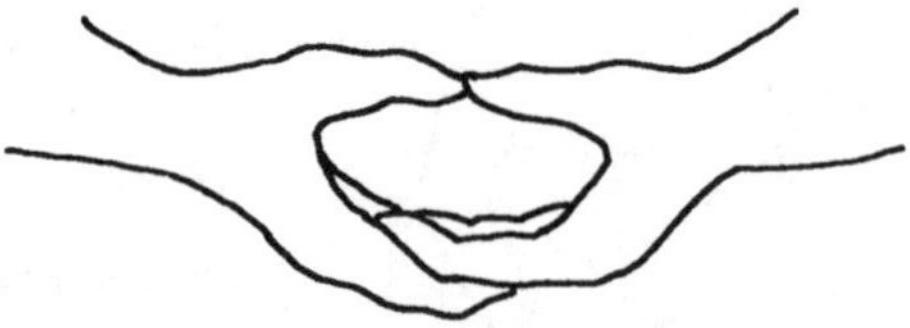

FIGURE 9

Cosmic mudra

your palms. This is called the cosmic mudra (see figure 9). Keeping your eyes open, look at the wall and drop your line of vision slightly.[17]

Once you have taken the zazen position, open your mouth and exhale deeply. This will help change your whole frame of mind. In order to work out the stiffness in your joints and muscles, slowly swing two or three times to the left and right, finally settling in an unmoving, upright posture. Once you are still, breathe quietly through your nose. The important thing here is to breathe naturally from the *tanden,* an area in your belly a little below the navel. Allow long breaths to be long and short breaths to be short, rather than trying to control each one. Do not force your breathing or make noise by breathing heavily.[18] The zazen posture is a marvelous posture because it is the best one for throwing out our petty human thoughts.

You will easily understand what I mean if you compare the zazen posture to Rodin's famous statue *The Thinker* (see figure 10). The figure sits hunched over, his shoulders drawn forward and his chest compressed, in a posture of chasing after illusions. The arms and legs are bent, the neck and fingers are bent, and even the toes are curled. When our body is bent and contorted like this, bloodflow and breathing become congested; we get caught up in our imagination and are unable to break free. On the other hand, when we sit zazen everything is straight—trunk, back, neck, and head. Because our abdomen rests comfortably on solidly folded legs, blood circulates freely toward the abdomen, and breath moves easily toward the *tanden.* Congestion is alleviated, excitability is lessened, and we no longer need to chase after fantasies and delusions. Doing correct zazen means taking the correct posture and entrusting everything to it.

FIGURE 10

The Thinker caught up in delusion, and the Sitter letting thought go

It is easy to tell you to aim at the correct posture and leave everything up to that, but it is not so simple to do. Even while we are in the zazen position, if we continue our thoughts, we are thinking and no longer doing zazen. Zazen is not thinking; nor is it sleeping. Doing zazen is to be full of life aiming at holding a correct zazen posture. If we become sleepy while doing zazen, our energy becomes dissipated and our body becomes limp. If we pursue our thoughts, our posture will become stiff. Zazen is neither being limp and lifeless nor being stiff; our posture must be full of life and energy.

This applies to any kind of activity. If you get sleepy while driving or working, your life force gets dull; if you worry, you get tense and rigid; both are dangerous. This is equally true for everyone, whether one is a statesman, a ditch digger, or a Zen priest. Our life force should be neither stagnant nor stiff. The most essential thing is that our life force live to its fullest potential. Zazen is the most condensed form of *life functioning as wide-awake life*. It's the practice that directly and purely manifests that life. So, although it is easy to explain, actually practicing this is the most crucial thing in our life and, at the same time, a tremendous task.

When we actually do zazen, we should be neither sleeping nor caught up in our own thoughts. We should be wide awake, aiming at the correct posture with our flesh and bones. Can we ever attain this? Is there such a thing as succeeding or hitting the mark? Here is where zazen becomes unfathomable. In zazen we have to vividly aim at holding the correct posture, yet there is no mark to hit! Or at any rate, the person who is doing zazen never perceives whether he has hit the mark or not. If the person doing zazen thinks his zazen is really getting good, or that he has "hit the mark," he is merely *thinking* his zazen is good, while actually he has become separated from the reality of his zazen. Therefore, we must always aim at doing correct zazen, without being concerned with perceiving the mark as having been hit.

This seems like a strange contradiction. Generally, most people think that as long as there is an aim, it is only natural that there will be a target to hit: precisely because there is a target, we can take aim. However, if we know that there isn't a target, why attempt to aim? This is the usual idea about give-and-take, ordinary calculating behavior. However, when we do zazen we have to let go of our self-centeredness and our dealings in relation to others. Zazen is just our *whole self doing itself by itself*. Zazen does zazen! Zazen is the act of throwing away the calculating way of thinking that supposes that as long as there is an aim there must be a target. We just sit in the midst of this contradiction where although we aim, we can never perceive hitting the mark. We just sit in the midst of this contradiction that is absolutely ridiculous when we think about it with our small mind. When we practice this kind of zazen and just sit, how indefinite we may feel![19] How unsatisfied or completely lost we may feel.

This seeming problem is exactly why zazen is so wonderful. This small self, this foolish self, easily becomes satisfied or complacent. We need to see complacency for what it is: just a continuation of the thoughts of our foolish self. However, in our zazen, it is precisely at the point where our small, foolish self remains unsatisfied, or completely bewildered, that immeasurable natural life beyond the thoughts of that self takes place. Life functions and the power of buddha is actualized, precisely at the point where we become completely lost.

People who practice zazen must understand intellectually beforehand just what it is, and then when actually sitting zazen, must just aim at the correct posture—not with their heads, but with their muscles and bones. Finally, they must drop everything and entrust everything to the correct zazen posture. Zazen actualizes the reality of the life of the self, just as it is. But there is no reason to think that we will perceive it.[20] It is impossible to look directly with our own naked eyes at the genuine or preconceptual reality of our own face. In this case, we must realize that it is only our calculating mind that is unsatisfied because it cannot see the results of its activity.

In any event, zazen is the best posture for truly aiming at reality as it is. Aiming at this posture of body and life, as it is, is also referred to as *shikantaza*—just sitting.[21]

My teacher Kōdō Sawaki Roshi often used to say, "Just do zazen, that's all." This is the same as "Zazen is the dharma, the dharma is zazen," and "Doing zazen is just doing zazen."

Just doing zazen is all there is to do. But there is a great deal of doubt about what that is, so many people find it difficult to develop a correct practice. My purpose throughout this book is to try to explain just what zazen is. However, please understand that there is no overall conclusion for this book other than what I have just said—that is, to actually do zazen.

Letting Go of Thoughts

I have said that if you sit and think during zazen, then that is thinking and not doing zazen. Does that mean no thoughts at all should occur to us during zazen? Is good zazen that condition when all thoughts have ceased to come into our minds?

Here we have to clearly distinguish "chasing after thoughts and thinking" from "ideas or thoughts merely occurring." If a thought occurs during zazen and we proceed to chase after it, then we are thinking and not doing zazen. Yet this doesn't mean that we are doing zazen only when thoughts have entirely ceased to occur. How should we understand this contradiction?

Imagine placing a large rock next to a person doing zazen. Since this rock is not alive, no matter how long it sits there, a thought will never occur to it. Unlike the rock, however, the person doing zazen next to it is a living human being. Even if we sit as stationary as the rock, we cannot say that no thoughts will occur. On the contrary, if they did not, we would have to say that that person is no longer alive. Of course, the truth of life never means to become lifeless like the rock. For that reason, thoughts ceasing to occur is not the ideal state of one sitting zazen. It is perfectly natural that thoughts occur. Yet, if we chase after thoughts, we are thinking and no longer doing zazen. So what should our attitude be?

Briefly, our attitude in zazen is aiming at maintaining the posture of zazen with our flesh and bones, and with our mind letting go of thoughts.[22]

What is letting go of thoughts? Well, when we think, we think of *something*. Thinking of something means grasping that something with thought. However, during zazen we open the hand of thought that is trying to grasp something, and simply refrain from grasping. This is letting go of thoughts.

When a thought of something does actually arise, as long as the thought does not grasp that something, nothing will be formed. For example, even if thought A ("a flower") occurs, as long as it is not followed by thought B ("is beautiful"), no meaning such as $A B$ ("a flower is beautiful") is formed. Neither is it something that could be taken in the sense of A *which is* B ("beautiful flower"). So, even if thought A does *occur*, as long as the thought does not *continue*, A occurs prior to the formation of a meaningful sequence. It is not measurable in terms of meaning, and it will disappear as consciousness flows on.

Since in zazen blood recedes from the head and excitability is lessened, zazen is by nature a posture in which we see the futility of chasing after thoughts. As long as we entrust everything to the zazen posture, opening the hand of thought will come naturally and spontaneously. Again, however, human life is not a machine, so even in the zazen posture it is possible to think as much as we like. So the essential point when doing zazen is to aim, full of life, at the posture of zazen with our flesh and bones while at the same time leaving everything up to the posture and letting go of thoughts. By aiming at the zazen posture and simultaneously opening the hand of thought, both body and mind do zazen in the proper spirit. Zazen is not something we *think* about doing wholeheartedly—-it is something we actually practice.

Dōgen, quoting the Chinese master Yaoshan Weiyan (called in Japanese Yakusan Igen), called this the *thought of no thought*.[23] While doing zazen with our flesh and bones, we aim at (think) letting go of thoughts (no thought). Later, Keizan Jōkin Zenji coined the expression *kakusoku,* which means being wide awake actually living out reality.[24]

As Keizan's expression *kakusoku* states admirably the mental attitude of a person doing zazen, I will talk about the conditions during zazen by using the words "wake up" in this sense. This word *kakusoku* might be equally understood to mean *reality waking up as reality*. At any rate, this "waking up" is different from cognizing or perceiving, and this difference is crucial. Knowing and perceiving imply a dichotomy, a confrontation between the thing that knows and the thing that is known.

We are at all times and in every situation living out the reality of our own lives, whether we believe it to be so or not. Never-theless, we lose sight of this. We doze off or start thinking, and thus we cause this reality to appear dull and foggy. It's just like driving a car when we are either sleepy or absorbed in thought. Our life, like our driving, becomes careless and hazardous. "Waking up" means to let go of thoughts—that is, we wake up from sleep or thought and perform the reality of the zazen posture that we are practicing with our flesh and bones. In other words, it is with our flesh and bones that we actualize the reality of the self.[25]

Waking Up to Life

What actually goes on in the internal experience of doing zazen? An analytical description of it is difficult, but that is exactly what I will try to do. First of all, consider a line ZZ'. This line represents truly maintaining the zazen posture (see figure 11). When we are doing zazen, this line ZZ' is the reality of our lives right now, so we make every effort to keep to it. But we are not fixed and unmoving the way rocks are, so it happens that we tend to drift away from this line: thoughts come up or we doze off.

When a thought comes into our mind and we move away from the steadiness that line ZZ represents in the figure, if we take this thought a as a basis and continue with thoughts a' and a'', we are thinking. If something about our work comes to mind and we continue with thoughts about the arrangements and management of the work, we are clearly doing nothing but thinking about our work. Then we open the hand of thought and let the thoughts go, and we wake up to the posture of zazen with our flesh and bones. We return to the reality of life. This waking up is the arrow pointing back down to line ZZ'.

But after a while we become drowsy. This is b. If this b continues on to b' and b'', we are actually dozing. Perhaps it seems strange to use this progression of symbols, b, b', and b'', for dozing, too, but in actually doing zazen, that is the way it is. Thinking and sleeping in zazen are pretty much the same. When we get sleepy, a drowsy thought b wafts into our mind, and then without our noticing it another sleepy thought b' slides in on its heels. Thus, when we become sleepy during zazen and some thought floats into our head, that is nothing but dreaming. If a thought comes to mind while we are wide awake and we chase after it, this is called *thinking*. And, if a thought comes to mind when we are sleepy and we drift after it, we are simply chasing after a dream in our sleep. Or we may be nodding away and at the same time *thinking* that although we are sleepy we are holding out and sitting as solidly as ever. What we are really doing here is just dreaming about doing zazen.

In actually doing zazen, there is no difference between chasing after thoughts and sleeping—at least speaking from my experience of zazen this is the case. Therefore, when we become sleepy during zazen, we have to wake up by vigorously putting our energy into our sitting with our flesh and bones and cease chasing after thoughts. We have to "wake up" and return to the reality of life, which can also be expressed by an arrow pointing up to ZZ'.

Sometimes we completely forget about where we are and what we are doing. We may chase after thoughts c, c', c'', and end up completely separated from the reality of our life of doing zazen right now. Without being aware of it, we may start associating with or carrying on a dialogue with some vivid figure c''' that has been totally fabricated within our own act of chasing after thoughts. Even at a time like this, if we wake up—that is, actually perform the posture of zazen with our flesh and bones and open the hand of our thoughts—this very lifelike phantom c''' will disappear instantly and we will be able to return to the reality of zazen (ZZ'). This is a truly remarkable point. It makes us realize clearly that our fantasy c''' has no reality and that it is nothing but the empty coming and going of thoughts. Noticing things like this during zazen, whether it is at stage c, c', c'', or c''', we should wake up to zazen as soon as possible and return to ZZ'.

Actually, zazen is not just being somehow glued to line ZZ'. Doing zazen is a continuation of this kind of returning up from sleepiness and down from chasing after thoughts. That is, the posture

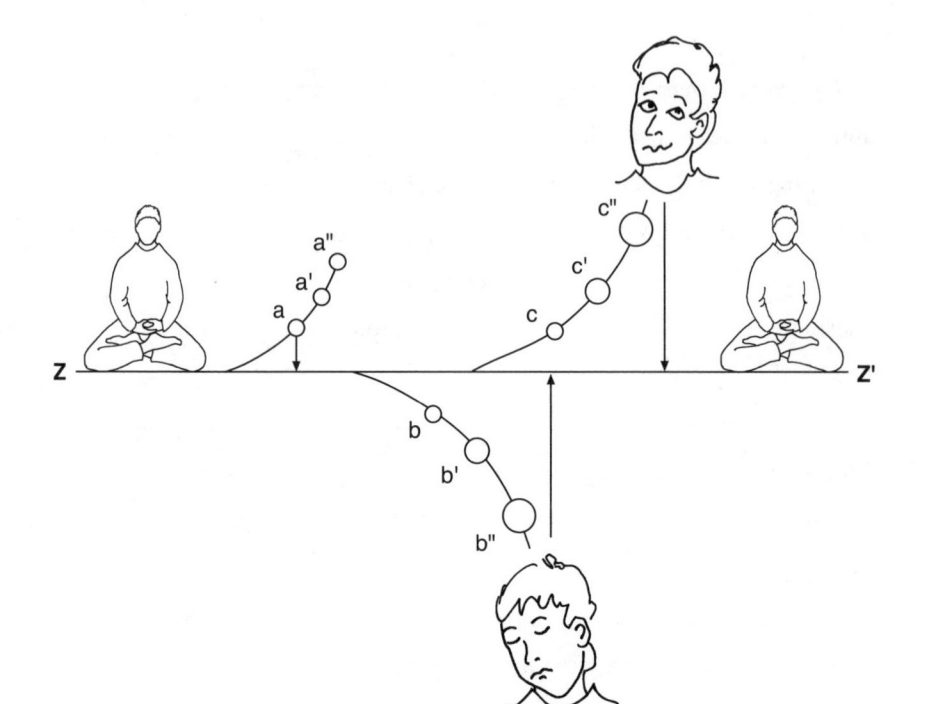

FIGURE 11

The mind in zazen

of waking up and returning to ZZ' at any time is itself zazen. This
is one of the most vital points regarding zazen. When we are doing
zazen line ZZ', or just doing zazen, represents our reality, so it is
essential to maintain that line. Actually, ZZ' represents the reality
of the posture of zazen, but the reality of our life is not just ZZ'. If
it were only ZZ', we would be as unchanging and lifeless as a rock!
Although we aim at the line ZZ', we can never actually adhere to it,
because it (ZZ') does not exist by itself. Nevertheless, we keep aiming at ZZ', because it is through clinging to thoughts that we keep
veering away from it. The very power to wake up to ZZ' and return
to it is the reality of the life of zazen.

Zazen enables us to realize that all the thoughts that float into our heads are nothing but empty comings and goings that have no real substance and vanish in a moment. Yongjia's poem *The Song of Enlightenment* (Ch. *Zhengddaoge;* Jp. *Shōdōka*) puts it this way:

The five elements of existence are just clouds floating
  aimlessly to and fro,
While the three poisons are but bubbles that appear
  and vanish.
When reality is seen, neither subject nor object exists,
And in a moment a hellish destiny is averted.[26]

Truly, all thoughts, delusions, and cravings are like bubbles and are nothing but empty comings and goings that lose their appearance of substance when we wake up in zazen. Even a hellish realm, developed by our own thoughts and fantasies, is eradicated in an instant. Zazen enables us to experience this as reality. The reason I have taken it upon myself to try to explain with diagrams what is actually happening during zazen is this: people tend to think that doing zazen means to aim at the line *ZZ '*, to train and discipline their minds, and finally to hold unwaveringly to *ZZ '* itself. I wish to make it clear that zazen as real life—the zazen that Dōgen Zenji called "the directly transmitted zazen of the buddhas and patriarchs"—is not like that. Consider the following passage from Dōgen Zenji's *Eihei Kōroku*.

The Patriarch Nagarjuna spoke thus: Zazen is the dharma of all the buddhas. Non-Buddhists also practice zazen. However, they make the mistake of coloring it; their incorrect views are like thorns. Therefore, it cannot be the same as the zazen of the buddhas and bodhisattvas. Sravakas and pratyeka buddhas also do zazen, but they wish only to control their minds and seek to reach nirvana. This is not the same as the zazen of the buddhas and bodhisattvas.[27]

These words of Nagarjuna, who lived about 150 to 250 C.E., were quoted by Dōgen Zenji in the thirteenth century. Nagarjuna had already made clear the difference between the zazen of the buddhas and bodhisattvas and the meditation practices of non-Buddhist practitioners and Buddhists seeking only their own salvation, which he labeled *hinayana* (a small-minded attitude, literally "small vehicle").[28] The meditation practices of non-Buddhists are not the pure zazen of life itself. They are flavored or colored with various kinds of profit and are developed from a worldly and utilitarian outlook. *Sravakas* and *pratyeka buddhas* meditate in order to gradually decrease delusion and craving, finally seeking to extinguish them entirely and enter nirvana. Neither of these is the zazen that has been correctly transmitted by the buddhas and ancestors.

In other words, the zazen we do is not something at which we succeed only when we become one with *ZZ '*, as in the drawing we have been considering. Decreasing delusion and desire and finally extinguishing them completely is not the purpose of zazen.

Some Buddhists say nirvana (enlightenment) is the complete extinction of delusion and craving, and zazen or meditation is practiced in order to reach this state. However, if we assume this type of enlightenment to be the truth of human life, then this is nothing but saying that the truth of life is lifelessness, or death! Since cravings existing in human life are the cause of suffering, such Buddhists struggle to extinguish them and attain the bliss of nirvana. But isn't seeking to get rid of pain and to attain the bliss of nirvana itself a desire or craving? Actually, this too is craving, and precisely because of that the practitioner is caught in self-contradiction and can't escape suffering.[29] This is why Dōgen Zenji said, "The practice of the buddhas and patriarchs is completely different from the way of *hinayana*," and it is why he quoted from an earlier ancestor about not trying to follow a limited form of zazen as self-control.

The zazen of the buddhas and ancestors, the zazen of the reality of life, is not like this. Since desires and cravings are actually a manifestation of the life force, there is no reason to hate them and try to extinguish them. And yet, if we become dragged around by them and chase after them, then our life becomes fogged over.[30] The important point here is not to cause life to be fogged over by thought based on desires or cravings, but to see all thoughts and desires as resting on the foundation of life, to let them be as they are yet not be dragged around by them.[31] It is not a matter of making a great effort not to be dragged around by desires. It is just waking up and returning to the reality of life that is essential. If we apply this to zazen, it means that, even if various thoughts like a and b do occur, they will all vanish when we wake up to zazen.

Even when one is completely off track, carried away to the point where c''' appears as a very vivid image, by waking up to zazen even c''' will disappear in an instant. Anyone who does zazen is actually enabled to experience with her whole body that thoughts are nothing but empty comings and goings without any independent or unchanging substance. However, unless we actually practice zazen, this is very difficult to understand.

I realize that to say you cannot understand this without doing zazen may sound presumptuous. I say this because usually we are unable to recognize that what we think about is nothing but empty comings and goings, due to plunging our heads too far into our thoughts and living too much in the world of thought. Once we think of something we want or like, we assume that the simple fact of thinking we want it or like it is the truth. Then, since we think this idea is the truth and is worth seeking, we proceed to chase after it everywhere and our whole world becomes a world of greed. On the other hand, once we think of something we hate or dislike, we assume again that the simple fact of thinking we hate it is the truth. Thinking that this idea is the truth so we ought to follow it, we chase after it until our whole world turns into anger.[32]

The activities in our everyday lives are almost entirely the result of chasing after ideas this way, causing vivid lifelike images to become fixed in our mind, and then giving more and more weight to these fixed delusions and desires until finally we get carried away by them.[33] It would be even more accurate to say that ordinarily we are being flung about by desire and delusion without even knowing it. It is like a man who is drinking saké (consuming fantasies). At first he knows that he is getting drunk, but when he gets to the stage where the saké is drinking the man, then he is adrift in fantasies without even knowing it, and he acts accordingly. Almost all people and societies throughout the world today are carried away by desire and delusion. This is precisely why our zazen comes to have such a great significance. When we wake up during zazen we are truly forced to experience the fact that all the things we develop in our thoughts vanish in an instant.

Despite the fact that we almost always stress the content of our thoughts, when we wake up, we wake up to the reality of life and make this reality our center of gravity. It is at this time that we clearly realize that all the desires and delusions within our thoughts are substantially nothing. When this kind of zazen experience fully becomes a part of us, even in our daily lives, we will not be carried away by the comings and goings of various images, and we will be able to wake up to our own lives and begin completely afresh from the reality of life.

So are desires, delusions, and thoughts like *a, b,* and *c* all things that primarily do not exist and should be denied? Of course not, because as I mentioned before, even thoughts, which produce desire and delusion, are a manifestation of the power of life. Yet if we continue the thought and become carried away by desire and delusion, life becomes obscured and stifled. So we wake up to *ZZ'* and from this standpoint of waking up we are able to see that thoughts, desires, and delusions are all the scenery of life. During zazen, they are the scenery of zazen.

There is scenery only where there is life. While we are living in this world, there will be happiness and unhappiness, favorable and adverse conditions, interesting and boring things. There will be pleasant times and painful times, times to laugh and times to be sad. All of these are part of the scenery of life. Because we plunge into this scenery, become carried away by it, and end up running helter-skelter, we become frantic and we suffer. In zazen, even though various lifelike images appear to us, we are able to see this scenery of life for what it is by waking up to *ZZ'*.

This is important to consider in regard to the "I" that is determined by relationships with "the other." The "I" ruled from the outside is scenery in the life of the self. It is not that there is no such thing as an "I" fixed from the outside. There is, and it produces all sorts of scenery. But my own true life is the reality of life that I wake up to without being carried away by the scenery. Zazen is the foundation of life where this reality of life is being manifested. In that sense, zazen is the reality of the self—the true self.[34] The essential thing in zazen is not to eliminate delusion and craving and become one with ZZ'. Of course there are times like this during zazen, but this, too, is just part of the scenery of zazen. We aim at ZZ' even though we have a tendency to diverge from it. The very attitude of returning to ZZ' and waking up is most important for practicing zazen as the foundation of life.

FOUR

The World of Intensive Practice

Sesshins Without Toys

I want to clarify further the actuality of zazen and our life attitude in accord with zazen by looking at intensive Zen retreats, *sesshins,* and what is experienced through them. The word *sesshin* means "to touch or listen to the mind," and sesshins consist of several days dedicated almost entirely to zazen.[35]

After my teacher Sawaki Roshi's death in 1965, I began to do sesshins at Antaiji for five days every month. There are no sesshins in February, however, due to the cold, nor in August, due to the heat, and the July and September sesshins are only three days long. In all of these sesshins the schedule consists simply of a repetition of fourteen periods of zazen interspersed with briefer periods of Zen walking meditation *(kinhin),* from four o'clock in the morning until nine in the evening. There are three meals a day and a half-hour break after each one, when everyone attends to personal needs.

At Antaiji each period of zazen is fifty minutes long, while at many other monasteries and centers the periods are thirty or forty minutes. There are two unique characteristics of Antaiji sesshins. One is that there is absolutely no talking. There are no greetings or socializing, and not even any of the sutra-chanting that might happen at other times in a temple. Usually the head of a Soto Zen temple does not face the wall but rather faces the rest of the monks or practitioners to watch over them, but I always face the wall along with everyone else. These are the main characteristics of Antaiji sesshins. The only instruction added to these rules is that you apply yourself to your own practice regardless of anyone else. I began this style of sesshin after experiencing various types of sesshins, and I have continued this practice since 1965 because I believe it to be the purest way of putting into practice the words of Sawaki Roshi: "Zazen is the self doing itself by itself."

The five days of absolute silence are to help everyone become their self that is nothing but universal self without socializing or diverting their attention to others.[36] Moreover, this uninterrupted silence makes the five days into one continuous period of zazen. We don't use the *kyōsaku,* a stick used in many Zen temples to wake up a sitter who might have dozed off. Since we set everything aside and face the wall, just being ourselves during zazen, we may feel a terrible boredom. If the *kyōsaku* were carried around, it would become a toy to divert people from their boredom. For example, someone sitting quietly might hear a person carrying a *kyōsaku* around and begin to think about how perfect their posture is and why there is no reason for them to get hit, or about how long the afternoon is and how they could arrange to get hit just to pass the time.

It seems to me that we spend all our lives playing with toys. It begins as soon as we are born. The first toy is the nipple of the milk bottle. When we are a little older, we turn to dolls and teddy bears. After that, it's do-it-yourself kits, cameras, and cars. At adolescence, we move on to sex, and then come study and research, competition and sports, along with earnestness in business and perhaps the search for fame. This is all just playing with toys! Right up to our death, we exchange one toy for another, and we end our lives having done nothing but play with toys.

Doing zazen means to actualize the reality of life. Zazen is *the self which is only the self of the universe,* without any playing with toys. Zazen is like the time just before our death when all the toys have been taken away. Yet, even then, we look around for something to play with, if only for an instant.

What do you do if you get sleepy during a sesshin at Antaiji? If the purpose of the *kyōsaku* is to clear away your sleepiness, you can't help but fall asleep when it isn't being used. However, there is no need to worry—there is absolutely no one who sleeps through the entire seventy hours of zazen in a five-day sesshin! Inevitably, you wake up. Since it is your own practice, you just do zazen wholeheartedly. Zazen is not something a person should be forced to do. It's a practice you do yourself, as the self which is only the self.

There may be an occasion when you are awake but very bored. In order to pass the time, you may think about one certain thing and entertain yourself with this idea. Even though this is your own practice, it is ridiculous to pass the time like this, but occasionally people do. If you are mentally normal, however, you will not be able to keep this fantasizing up indefinitely—at a sesshin where there is only silence and long continuous hours of zazen, you'd feel like you were going crazy. A healthy mind cannot bear to struggle with and relate to one deluded thought over a long period of time. In the end, you will realize by yourself that the most comfortable thing is to let go of delusions and aim at a solid zazen posture. In other words, these sesshins are just sitting as self which is only self, without any outside restrictions. Consequently, you cannot help but return to that self which is only self, only life happening here and now, and which is unmoved by delusive thoughts.

As I've said, I sit facing the wall, like everyone else in the zazen hall. This does away with a relationship between us based on a watcher and those watched. If I sat with the intention of keeping watch on everyone else, then that is all I would be doing, and I would lose sight of my own zazen. Also, if everyone were conscious of being watched while doing zazen, it would become a zazen carried on within the dichotomy of "self" and "other" and would no longer be zazen that is truly the self which is only self. I have to carry on my own zazen practice, while everyone else has to practice his or her own zazen as self which is only true self.

There is no instruction given regarding zazen during sesshin, so to do a sesshin like this properly you have to have already understood what your mental attitude should be. I hope people will sit sesshins after having read and understood this. If they still have questions, they can visit a Zen teacher and ask their questions at times other than during sesshin.

A person who decides to do zazen after reading my explanation has quite a different attitude from one who might just come and sit zazen unquestioningly. There are also many people who are concerned with intellectual understanding—that is, they are full of argumentative theories. In order that these opinionated people may understand through their own experience that zazen is not theo-ry—it is something you actually do—I have them dive right into this totally silent zazen practice.

Before Time and "I" Effort

When we do this kind of sesshin, we become aware of various truths as personal experience, not theory. The first thing we can't help but feel when sitting these sesshins is the tremendous drawing out of time. Of sesshin it is said that "A day is as long as eternity" and "A day is long as it seemed in one's childhood." How often in our day-to-day life do we share a joke with a friend or perhaps watch a bit of televi-sion and, before we know it, half the day or perhaps even the whole day has passed. But when we sit zazen the entire day, time just does not pass easily. Our legs hurt and we become filled with boredom, and there is nothing else to do but live out time as the reality of life, moment by moment.

During sesshin all our activities are regulated by a bell. Two gongs sound, and we all stand up from zazen and begin walking. Doing *kinhin,* the thought arises of how fed up we already are with zazen, and then, discouragingly, we realize that it is still the morning of the second day and less than half the sesshin is over. I'm sure that everyone doing sesshin has had this kind of thought.

How in the world do we get through the remaining time? Arriving at this point, we just have to transcend time. If we don't forget this thing called time, it will be impossible for us to continue through all the rest of the hours of the sesshin.[37]

When we transcend time, or forget time, we actually meet the fresh reality of life. Time exists for us because we compare one moment with another, and in the welter of perception we feel time flowing swiftly. When we no longer compare, and just be that self which is nothing but self, then we are able to transcend this swiftness or comparison that we call time. Those who continue sitting sesshin no longer recall time. Simply hearing three gongs, you begin zazen; if it's two gongs, then kinhin. Another three gongs signal that it is time to sit again; then two gongs and it's back to kinhin. We just continue the sesshin as it is, following the signals of the bell.[38] No one thinks about whether it is a long time or a short time. Finally, without thinking about it, five days have passed and the sesshin is over. Only then do we notice we have completely forgotten time while doing zazen, though I'm afraid that such an expression may invite serious misunderstanding. It may be more appropriate to say that, just applying ourselves to zazen, five days have passed all by themselves.[39] Actually, no matter what words we use, nothing is really appropriate. We simply have to experience a sesshin personally.

This kind of experience actually shows us just what time is, as well as what *before time* is. Ordinarily, we take it for granted that we all live in time, but through sesshin we are able to experience directly that this is not so. Rather, it is the life of the self that creates the appearance of time.

When we do zazen, we fold our legs and sit without moving, keeping perfectly still. So you would have to say it is painful, compared with a self-indulgent way of life in which we are usually able to move around as we wish. However, if we begin to think during zazen about how painful it is and how we are persevering and bearing that pain, we will never be able to sit quietly throughout the whole five days. We might be able to do a couple of hours of zazen, or even four or five, strictly on our ability to persevere and endure pain, but there is no way we could ever sit a five-day sesshin simply by persevering. Furthermore, we could never sit through a sesshin every single month or lead a life of zazen practice by virtue of some egotistical idea about our ability to endure pain. And even if we were able to do so, it would be utterly meaningless! We would only be comparing our own ability to discipline ourselves and persevere with that of others, and zazen would become nothing but an extension of our disposition to compare ourselves with other people. The most important thing during sesshin is to throw away even these ideas of how painful it is or how we are persevering amid pain, and become submerged in zazen as it is, as the *self doing itself by itself*. Only by sitting still and leaving everything up to the posture will time pass of its own accord. Only when we throw away our ideas of pain and perseverance will we be able to sit a sesshin without anxiety.

Through sesshins, we are actually made to experience what it means to have the bottom fall out of our thoughts of persevering and suffering. This has an enormous influence in our daily lives. We meet many problems and misfortunes in our day-to-day affairs, but what usually happens is that in confronting a problem we begin to struggle. And by doing so, we force ourselves into an even worse situation. This is easy to see when it concerns someone else. When others have fallen into unfortunate circumstances, as observers we often say they should "just stop struggling" or "just calm down." As observers, we can very coolly say this, but when the trouble is our own, we suddenly lose our ability to stay calm. How can we make this self—which can't help but struggle—stop struggling and settle down? There is no way unless the bottom of our thoughts about our suffering and our persevering falls out.[40] During sesshins we are made to experience exactly that. Sesshin is the practice we carry on prior to the distinction of one's own power and the power of others, prior to time, and prior to persevering.

The Scenery of Life

Satori and Zen seem to have such an intimate relationship in Japan that when somebody says "satori," everybody immediately associates it with Zen, and vice versa. People who begin to sit sesshin often wonder, "When we do zazen, don't we need to have a satori experience?" In the West, the word "enlightenment" has the same effect. Truly though, satori is inexplicable, and it would be safer not to bring it up at all. I say this because people usually speak of *satori* in contrast to *delusion,* and the distinction between satori and delusion is nothing but a comparison that we set up in our ordinary minds.

The true satori of Shakyamuni Buddha is not like this. It is said that Shakyamuni made the following statement upon attaining satori: "I attained the way simultaneously with the whole world and all sentient beings. Everything—mountains, rivers, trees, grasses—all attained buddhahood."

For Shakyamuni, satori wasn't something peculiar only to himself. His was the satori of life inclusive of himself and all things. That is something that truly goes beyond the discrimination of our ordinary minds. In the Heart Sutra *(Prajna Paramita Hridaya Sutra)* it says, "There is no birth or death, no purity or impurity, no increase or decrease." Satori is beyond birth and death, beyond increase (gain) and decrease (loss), beyond impurity (delusion) and purity (satori). How can satori be beyond satori? This is a very important point. Satori related to delusion is a limited kind of "satori" based on comparing one thing with another. True satori is not based on such discriminations in our mind, it belongs to the whole of life. This kind of satori means to be enlightened to the reality of life prior to the distinctions of self and other, or delusion and satori.

If we wish to say that we have gained satori as a result of our practice, we should remember well that such satori belongs to the realm of the ego. It is nothing but a satori based on a distinction drawn between yourself and others. It is nothing but a discussion about the world created by the discrimination of our ordinary minds.

In *Only Buddha Together with Buddha (Shōbōgenzō: Yuibutsu-yobutsu)*, Dōgen Zenji writes, "If satori arises from any preconception of satori, that satori will not be reliable. True satori does not rely on concepts of satori, but comes from far beyond conceptualization. Satori is grounded only in satori itself and is assisted only by the power of satori itself. Know that delusion as some fixed thing does not exist. Know that satori is not an entity that exists."

A student came to see me and asked me this: "When we do zazen in sesshin, there are times when no matter how much we try to stop chasing thoughts and put our energy into the zazen posture, thoughts just keep coming one after another, and we can't help but chase after them. But at other times, we can do zazen with a completely clear mind without any thoughts coming up. Wouldn't you call this satori or *kenshō?*"

I replied, "Certainly when we do sesshins, we often have this experience. But if you call those times we can't help but chase thoughts *delusion,* and call clear-minded zazen *satori,* then delusion and satori are essentially like conditions caused by changes in temperature and humidity.

"We have all kinds of weather throughout the year, and even during a single sesshin the weather may go through changes. If we continue doing sesshins over a long period of time, we naturally see that there is a causal relationship between the temperature and humidity and our own psychological condition. For the most part, we begin to sense when certain conditions will arise. For example, when it is hot and muggy, no matter how much effort we try to put into sitting zazen, our heads simmer as though they were fermenting; there is nothing we can do about it. But when the air is dry and a cool evening breeze is blowing, our heads clear and it certainly feels as if we have become one with zazen. However, both of these are the conditions of our heads responding to the temperature and humidity. Since doing zazen means to sit and aim at being one with zazen, naturally this kind of zazen is very fine, although this doesn't mean that such zazen is *good,* and that zazen that isn't like this is a failure.

"Regardless of conditions, what is essential in doing zazen is just to sit, aiming at zazen and waking up to zazen. In just sitting and waking up to zazen, the various conditions going on in our heads simply become the scenery of our zazen!"[41] The student went off chuckling at my explanation that satori and delusion are conditions of temperature and humidity.

A few days later, the September sesshin began. As the early part of September is hot, the sesshin is only three days long. As usual, the first two days were very muggy and we were doing zazen soaked in sweat. But on the morning of the third day, it cooled off refreshingly and began to feel like fall. We were able to do zazen in comfort and on that note the sesshin ended. At the end of a sesshin everyone relaxes and we have tea together. At this time my student came back to the issue of weather and remarked that he had certainly experienced that satori and delusion are influenced by temperature and humidity.

The world we live in is not something that exists independently of our thoughts and ideas. Our world and these thoughts and ideas appear to us as a unified whole. Depending on what our thoughts and ideas are, our world may appear to us in completely different ways. These thoughts and feelings constitute our psychological condition. Moreover, our psychological condition is at the same time our physiological condition. When something breaks down inside of us physically, our minds no longer remain clear. And if our minds are not clear, then the eyes with which we see the world and our views of life become dark. Our lives and the whole world take on a gloomy appearance. On the other hand, when we feel healthy our minds brighten, and consequently our outlook on everything becomes brighter.

Furthermore, our physiological conditions are tremendously influenced by the environment in which we live. The changes and conditions of climate and weather both affect us. This cause-and-effect relationship is particularly easy to see when you lead a life as unvaried and devoid of distractions as the sesshins at Antaiji.

The essential matter here is the attitude of just striving to wake up regardless of the conditions you are in. It is not about arriving at some state where all thoughts have disappeared. To calmly sit amidst these cause-and-effect relationships without being carried away by them is *shikantaza.*

Like the weather, there are all sorts of conditions in our personal lives: clear days, cloudy days, rainy ones, and stormy ones. These are all waves produced by the power of nature and are not things over which we have control. No matter how much we fight against these waves, there is no way we can make a cloudy day clear up. Cloudy days are cloudy; clear days are clear. It is only natural that thoughts come and go and that psychological and physiological conditions fluctuate accordingly. All of this is the very reality and manifestation of life. Seeing all of this as the scenery of life, without being pulled apart by it—this is the stability of human life, this is settling down in our life.

This is the same as the zazen we do. We always try to sit zazen aiming at being steadily awake here and now, aiming at the line ZZ'. Yet it's not a matter of being able to adhere to ZZ', since we inevitably slide away from it. So we move away from ZZ' and then we wake up to ZZ'; we move away again and wake up to it again. Zazen is the very posture of forever waking up to ZZ'. As long as we have this attitude, all the thoughts that occur to us when we move away from ZZ'' become the scenery of zazen. The times when we can strictly maintain the line ZZ' are also the scenery of zazen. It is not that the cessation of all thought is satori and good, and the arising of thoughts and the tendency to chase after them is delusion and bad. Just sitting, transcending good or evil, satori or delusion, is the zazen that transcends the sage and the ordinary man.

In *The Record of Linji (Rinzai Roku)*, Linji Yixuan (Rinzai Gigen, d. 867) says:

> The true practitioner of the Way completely transcends all things. Even if heaven and earth were to tumble down, I would have no misgivings. Even if all the buddhas in the ten directions were to appear before me, I would not rejoice. Even if the three hells were to appear before me, I would have no fear. Why is this so? Because there is nothing to dislike.

For Rinzai, the appearance of all the buddhas in the past, present, and future was not something to rejoice over, nor was the appearance of the three hells something of which to be afraid. Of course, not being afraid of the appearance of some hell doesn't mean that for Rinzai hell had no existence. For him, hell was a kind of scenery that was different from the scenery of the buddhas. The point is that whether some hell, all the buddhas, or anything else appeared before him, Rinzai saw all of these as the scenery of his life. For us this is nothing but the scenery of our zazen.

I hope that people who practice zazen will continue regular sesshins and daily zazen for at least ten years. It's a tremendous thing to be able to give oneself to this kind of practice and not be caught up in distractions. Our deepest mental suffering will come up during these years of zazen, and we will be able to continue our practice only if we have the stability to see this suffering as the scenery of our life and not be carried away by it. Working through these ten years, we develop a posture of living out the reality of our true self.

If we lead this sort of life and sit zazen, at whatever age, there is no doubt that we will come to have a commanding view of who we are. When we live this way, not only zazen, but daily life itself, is such that we cannot find the value of our existence in what other people say or in things that we want. It is a life that is unbearable unless we discover the value of our existence within ourself.

What is essential is for us to live out the reality of our true self, whether we are doing one period of zazen, a five-day sesshin, or practicing for ten years or more.

Opening

the

Hand

of

Thought

—

74

FIVE

Zazen and the True Self

Universal Self

Our zazen is always *self doing self.* Does this mean zazen has no relationship to other people and things? Isn't this just ignoring society and other people, being caught up in self-fascination or withdrawal from the world? If zazen isn't closing oneself up in a shell, and is related to other people and society, just how is it related? I think it is only natural to be skeptical about this. This becomes a critical issue, especially for people who want to do zazen and are searching for a true way to live.

However, there is an even more basic question than the problem of self and others. A practitioner of zazen must ask, once again, just what "self" is. Only after taking a fresh look at self, and at the self/other relationship, will we be able to encounter the fundamental teaching of Mahayana Buddhism and the true attitude of zazen, which is the practice of that profound teaching. The background for our zazen must be the whole teaching of Buddhism, and the background of Buddhism must be our very own lives.

The problem of self and other is a good place to start. For "self," just what does "other" mean? Usually people think of "self" as something in opposition to "other," as *I* as opposed to *you*. This *I* is determined by external relationships with things defined as *other*. That is, *I* means that self which is not *other*. Conversely, *other* is always seen and defined by *me* and is something that is not myself.

Now, if *I* and *other* were diametrically opposed while at the same time dependent on each other, and we were to try to cut off this relationship with *other* and be *I which is only I,* this would certainly be a kind of withdrawal and escape from the world, or perhaps a kind of narcissism. It would be nothing but closing our eyes to our relationship with others and becoming self-satisfied.

Our zazen is not like this. Clearly, it is our thought, our thinking, that considers this contrasting relationship of "self" and "other" but when we are doing zazen we let go of this very thought. And, in doing so, we abandon this form of "self" and "other" as a contrasting relationship.

If we let go of this relationship in which "self" and "other" are diametrically opposed while at the same time mutually dependent, how can we talk about self any longer? Actually, during zazen we completely let go of this self-consciousness of an individual self defined by what is outside of us, yet it is right there that we wake up to all-inclusive self that is the reality of life. Even though we aren't conscious of this self and attach no name to it, it is self as raw living experience, self that is simultaneously personal and universal. To think that *universal self* is apart from *personal self* is just a limited comparison in the brain, just a variant of *self* versus *other*. Universal or all-inclusive self is free of comparisons and includes the personal self.

In other words, if I say "self which is only self," that expression does not refer to a self that excludes others while still being tied to them. It is not some sort of *I* distinct from *other*. "Self" is not some fixed concept regarding who you are, it is the all-inclusive self you personally wake up to. This self is the whole reality of life. Furthermore, the only thing we can wake up to as reality is the life of this whole self, and this is always *self which is only self*. This does not mean self-and-other completely disappears, but it differs radically from the usual self/other relationship. How does it differ and just what is a self/other relationship for people doing zazen?

The following story comes from the Edo period in Japan (1600–1868): Behind a temple there was a field where there were many squashes growing on a vine. One day a fight broke out among them, and the squashes split up into two groups, making a big racket shouting at one another. (See figures 12–14.)

The head priest heard the uproar and, stepping outside to see what was going on, found the squashes quarreling. The priest scolded them in a booming voice. "Hey, you squashes! What are you doing out there fighting? Everyone do zazen."

The priest taught them how to do zazen. "Fold your legs like this, sit up, and straighten your back and neck." While the squashes were sitting zazen in the way the priest had taught them, their anger subsided and they settled down.

Then the priest said quietly, "Everyone put your hand on top of your head." When the squashes felt the top of their heads, they found some weird thing attached there. It turned out to be the vine that connected them all together. "This is really strange. Here we've been arguing when actually we're all tied together and living just one life.[42] What a mistake! It's just as the priest said." After that, the squashes all got along with each other quite well.

FIGURE 12

Belligerent squashes

FIGURE 13

Squash zazen

FIGURE 14

Squashes living out the reality of life

To be sure, it is a fact that ordinarily we live as a small, individual body that we call "I." We think that this small, individual body is our self, imagining that we are this or that, but self as the reality of life is not simply this individual body. It has to be something more than that.

For example, the force that makes my heartbeat sends blood flowing through my whole body and allows me to breathe so many times per minute. It is not something that I control or activate. The power that performs these functions works completely beyond my thoughts. Can we say this power is not me because it comes from beyond my thinking mind? It is neither a "higher power" nor some "other power," nor is it my personal "self-power." It is the energy of life. As long as this power is working in me, it is surely the reality of my life.

This holds equally true for the thoughts and ideas that arise in my head. They are my thoughts, but the very power that allows them to arise transcends them by far. However, even while saying that this power is a transcendent power beyond my thoughts, as long as it is actually functioning within me, it is surely the reality of the life of the self functioning in and as me. While the reality of the life of the self exists beyond the thoughts of this individual, it is at the same time the very power actually functioning as this small individual.

Just as it is with me, so it is with you, too. The self as an individual entity, along with the contents of the various thoughts of this entity, takes for granted that each such entity is a self. And, in terms of the thoughts of each individual, they are indeed distinct. But the power of life that enables us to think in various ways, and that functions inside each individual, goes beyond the thoughts of this small *I*, and in this sense it is all-pervading. Just as in the story of the squashes that realized they were living out the reality of one life when they followed the vine attached to the top of their heads, we have to say that in this sense all existence, all living beings, are living out the power of one great all-pervading life.

Dōgen Zenji referred to this universal self of one all-pervading life as *jijuyū zanmai*, which means "freely receiving and functioning self" (literally, the samadhi of self-receiving-and-employing). Samadhi is the spirit of encountering all things with the same attitude, an attitude of evenness. *Jijuyū zanmai* is the samadhi of self receiving life and turning around to put it to work, to make it function. Since everything in and around us is constantly changing, we have to practice this samadhi inside and outside the zendo throughout our whole life. Everything that I have been talking about is nothing other than *jijuyū zanmai*, that is, zazen. Sitting zazen is the universal self sitting alone. Yet, at the same time, all things are the content or the scenery of that zazen or self. That is the meaning of *jijuyū zanmai*.

Sawaki Roshi used to describe zazen as "the self selfing the self." Usually people assume that they are born onto a stage or into a world that already exists, that they dance around on the stage for a while and then leave when they die. Actually, though, when I am born, I give birth to my world as well! I live together with that world; therefore, that world forms the contents of my self. Then, when I die, I take the world with me; that is, my world dies with me. That is the rationale behind Sawaki Roshi's noncommonsensical expression, "self selfing the self." I describe it as living out your own life through all the circumstances you may encounter. You give birth to, live out, and die together with your world. That is the reality of the life of the self, and to actually manifest the self that makes the self into the self is *jijuyū zanmai*. When we do zazen, we personally experience this clearly; we become nothing other than ourselves! Though we become nothing other than ourselves alone, the whole world is contained within that self.

People want things to go smoothly and try to avoid anything that involves suffering. Put simply, paradise is good, hell is bad. Actually, whether I am in heaven or hell I am living out my own life. Since both of them form the temporary scenery of my life, I am in no position to say I like paradise but don't like hell. If I fall into hell, then I have to acknowledge where I am and be willing to serve out my time there.

We are going to feel uneasy as long as we live a life of trying to get into heaven and avoid hell. It is vital to cultivate the spirit of living willingly in either situation. Ultimately, *jijuyū zanmai* is the one total act of living our whole life in a way that holds life most precious. I composed a short verse about this basic attitude:

Heaven or hell, love or hate,

No matter where I turn

I meet myself.

Holding life precious is

Just living with all intensity

Holding life precious.

During zazen we let go of our thoughts, which enables us to wake up to the undivided reality of life that pervades the whole universe.[43] Because we live within the thoughts of this small individual *I,* we are dragged about by them, and an *other* that is *not-I* closes in on us. When we let go of these thoughts and wake up to the reality of life that is working beyond them, we discover the self that is living universal nondual life, which pervades all living creatures and all existence.

From ancient times, Zen teachers have expressed this in various ways: original self, the self that pervades the ten-direction world, the self that fills the whole earth, or universal self.[44] In any event, whether we realize this or not, whether we practice it or not, we are all living the universal self. As I quoted earlier, when Shakyamuni attained enlightenment he said, "I attained the Way simultaneously with the whole world and all sentient beings." Everything—mountains, rivers, trees, grass—attained buddhahood. I think these words clearly show that what Shakyamuni became enlightened to was this universal self.

The Activity of the Reality of Life

All of us, regardless of whether we realize it or not, are living out the self as the whole universe. Since this is such a crucial point, I'll repeat it here. Usually we make the idea of the small individual self the center of our world and become firmly convinced that this small individual is our whole self, but this is not our true self.

The reality of life goes beyond my idea of myself as a small individual. Fundamentally, our self is living out nondual life that pervades all living things. This self is universal existence, everything that exists.[45] On the other hand, we usually lose sight of the reality of the life of universal self, clouding it over with thoughts originating from our small individual selves. When we let go of our thoughts, this reality of life becomes pure and clear. Living out this reality of life as it is—that is, waking up and practicing beyond thinking—is zazen. At this very point our basic attitude in practicing zazen becomes determined. The attitude of the practitioner in practicing zazen as a Mahayana Buddhist teaching never means to attempt to artificially create some new self by means of practice. Nor should it be aiming at decreasing delusion and finally eliminating it altogether. We practice zazen, neither aiming at having a special mystical experience nor trying to gain greater enlightenment. Zazen as true Mahayana teaching is always the whole self just truly being the whole self, life truly being life.

We all have eyes to see, but if we close them and say that the world is in darkness, how can we say that we are living out the true reality of life? If we open our eyes we see the sun is shining brilliantly. In the same way, when we live open-eyed and awake to life, we discover that we are living in the vigorous light of life. All the ideas of our small self are clouds that make the light of the universal self foggy and dull. Doing zazen, we let go of these ideas and open our eyes to the clarity of the vital life of universal self.

We discover the attitude of zazen as true Buddhism when we believe that the truth of this small self as an individual entity is universal self and actually practice the reality of life in zazen. This zazen is referred to as the activity of the reality of life.[46]

It can be said that in zazen we "believe and sit," but then we have to look at the meaning of "believe" in its Buddhist sense. Ordinarily, we use the word "believe" to mean thinking what someone has said is true. In religion when an agent of a god or God has said that there exists an invisible, metaphysical realm, that God has such and such powers, or that man has a soul, people have assumed it to be true and have acted accordingly. This has been called belief or faith. However, in Buddhism the fundamental definition of "belief" is totally different. It is clarity and purity.[47] In Buddhism "belief" does not mean to believe something in one's mind, such as that every person has an individual soul or that God exists outside us. Belief, in Buddhism, is to become clear and pure in actualizing the reality of universal life. We are in fact constantly living out life that pervades everything and goes beyond our individual thoughts, but we easily lose sight of this and become confused. We get carried away by the ideas of our small, individual self, just like the squashes that got carried away and started fighting. In zazen we let go of thoughts, lower our level of excitement, and live the universal self just truly being self. This is the basic meaning of belief, so the very act of doing zazen is an expression of our belief.

Most people have lost sight of reality so much that when we hear about universal self, we refuse to recognize it despite the fact that it refers to us. We assume that "universal life" must refer to someone else's life. However, when we hear that self is not some other person, that the truth of self is that we ourselves are living out the life that pervades all things, we may recognize that it is so. When we no longer doubt this, the second meaning of "belief" comes up, which is "no doubt." This is not a matter of hearing what somebody says and not doubting it. This has nothing to do with our own ideas and is so regardless of whether we believe it or doubt it. The meaning of "belief" in Buddhism is just not to doubt the simple truth that we are living out the reality of indivisible life.

A commentary on the Perfection of Wisdom teachings says, "We enter the great ocean of buddhadharma through faith."[48] The same can be said for our zazen. When one sits zazen actualizing or aiming at "the self which is the universe," that is doing zazen with faith. When the meaning of zazen is clarified as the activity of the reality of life, this is zazen that is true Buddhism.

In Buddhist sutras and commentaries, a vast number of words have been used to express this universal self, including suchness, buddha nature, mind, and nirvana.[49] One expression Dōgen Zenji used is "all-encompassing self," *jinissai jiko*.[50] If you run across any of these expressions while reading Buddhist texts, you should realize that they are all different names for the reality of life that we actually wake up to in zazen. You should realize that sutras are directly connected to your zazen and that they are meant to guide and teach you about the zazen you do. Throughout the history of Buddhism a great number of terms have been used to express the teaching in a variety of ways, eventually giving rise to the various traditions existing today. However, all of these expressions try to clarify that our true self is living out a life connected to all things, and so there is nothing else to do but to actualize and practice this all-connected life here and now.

One of the Buddhist traditions is the Pure Land school. According to this teaching, in the immeasurably far distant past there was a monk called Dharmakara, who made a great vow and practiced under a buddha named Lokesvararaja. He vowed that on the dawn of completing his practice and attaining buddhahood, he would create a wonderful pure buddha land. Furthermore, if there were any sentient beings who wished from the bottom of their hearts to enter this pure land, he would save them all without exception and take them there. Dharmakara actually did complete his practice; he became Amitabha Buddha. He then created the magnificent pure-land paradise just as he had vowed. Therefore, anyone who is totally disillusioned with this corrupt world, believes in this vow of Amitabha Buddha, earnestly desires to be born in the pure land, and chants his name will at that very moment be saved and reborn in the pure land simply by virtue of that deep faith.

This teaching of the Pure Land school looks completely different from the Zen school, in which one realizes satori within one's own zazen practice. In fact, it seems to be a teaching of salvation similar to Christianity. However, even Amitabha Buddha of the Pure Land school is just another name for universal self, here given the name of a buddha. Of course, Amitabha, also known as Amitayus, isn't the name of a person who actually existed historically. In Sanskrit, *amitabha* and *amitayus* mean "infinite light" and "immeasurable life." In other words, Amitabha Buddha is that life which connects all things.

If we analyze this Pure Land teaching, it looks something like this: Usually we get completely lost in the thoughts of our small, individualistic selves, but in terms of fundamental life that pervades everything, we are already saved by the vow of Amitabha Buddha. Believing in this vow and becoming clear and pure in Amitabha Buddha, we chant the phrase *"Namu amida butsu,"* "I put my faith in Amitabha Buddha." This is the phrase known as the *nembutsu*. This attitude is exactly the same as our attitude in doing zazen.[51]

In Buddhism, whether we do zazen or chant the *nembutsu,* our attitude toward these practices demonstrates the same attitude toward life. That is, Buddhism teaches us about this incomparable or absolute attitude toward life.

In other words, this small *I* is embraced by the immeasurable and boundless Amitabha Buddha. This has nothing to do with my small, limited thoughts of whether I think it is so or not. It does not depend on whether I believe it or not. I am, in fact, embraced and saved by the immeasurable and boundless Amitabha. Being thankful for this, I chant *Namu amida butsu.* When we say this with our mouths, we are expressing our deep sense of gratitude. When we perform it with our whole body, it is zazen as the activity of the reality of life, the zazen of believing and sitting. When people of the Pure Land school chant *Namu amida butsu,* they are doing zazen with their mouths, and when we do zazen, we are performing *Namu amida butsu* with our whole body.

In this sense, our zazen must always be the activity of just sitting, believing that life actualizes life through life, that buddha actualizes buddha through buddha, that self actualizes self through self.[51] We don't gradually become enlightened and eventually attain buddhahood by means of zazen. This small individual *I* we talk of will always be deluded, but regardless of that, zazen is buddha. We take the Buddha's posture with the body of this deluded being and throw ourselves into it. In the *Shōdōka,* it is expressed like this: "With one leap we immediately enter buddhahood."[52]

The World of
Self Unfolds

The Dissatisfactions of Modern Life

Western civilization has made enormous advances in science and technology, and has improved the efficiency of all kinds of work. Comparing it with past civilizations, where only a tiny elite were able to enjoy their lives, at the expense of so many others, it is easily arguable that our present-day civilization is by far the most prosperous of all. Moreover, many religious myths and pagan superstitions have been replaced by modern psychology and counseling to deal with the emotional and mental suffering that still trouble so many people. This is certainly something to be admired, and it leaves us trying to understand what role, if any, religion can play in all of this. Whether it be Buddhism, Christianity, Judaism, Islam, or any other religion in the world, a religion for this era must be able to identify and address the problems that cannot be solved by any amount of scientific progress. How

89

can people today find true peace, both internally as complete individuals and externally as members of a society?

We mostly take our so-called civilization for granted; and though most of us could not fashion a single board from a tree, move a single boulder, or mold a steel girder, still we live and work in fine houses and beautiful buildings. Moreover, most of us know nothing of how to spin a single thread of yarn, let alone how to weave a bolt of cloth, yet we wear the finest clothes and follow the fashions of the times. Most of us could not imagine harvesting a single grain of rice or wheat, yet we have never suffered from starvation. On top of all this, we surround ourselves with electrical appliances and other modern conveniences and live in great comfort. If we compare our situation to that of ancient Egyptian civilization, our lives would be comparable in luxury to that of a person served by dozens of slaves. We are kings who, through television, are entertained by the best performers in the country and, by modern transportation, are carried to our destinations at speeds the Egyptian pharaohs, borne on palanquins by slaves, couldn't even imagine.

Now that we have such a life, would you say we are living with no wants or discontentments, with complete peace of mind? Unfortunately not. On the contrary, most people today feel dissatisfied with their situation and run around trying to make more money, or enjoy an even higher standard of living, or go on strike for better wages. On a larger scale, countries are ever ready to wage war against one another for their national interests. In the future, if even greater technological advances mean people will have no material wants, do you think the discontent that causes national strife and international wars will also cease? If you do, you are being far too optimistic. The higher the standard of living a people achieve, the higher the level they want to reach. The more power a nation is able to gain, the more it tries to acquire. This spiral perpetuates itself because the knowledge to develop our standard of living, which is the wisdom of our modern scientific and technological civilization, was born in a matrix of dissatisfaction. Dissatisfaction is the mother of invention and progress. That is why no matter how much scientific or technological progress is made, people will never be satisfied. As long as they walk along this path shouldering the bag of desires and dissatisfaction, every time they open that bag, even hundreds or thousands of years from now, they will always be pulling out their dissatisfaction along with their new ideas.

That we make continuous scientific progress resulting in greater human comfort is fine, and that we possess the dissatisfaction that serves as the force for developing and progressing is also certainly a wonderful thing. The problem is that dissatisfaction with the present easily leads to impatience for our desires to be fulfilled, and that engenders a behavior of daggers drawn toward any and all competitors, resulting in the total loss of any peace in our lives.

In other words, no matter how far science progresses, it is not going to be the answer to our lack of peace of mind. No matter how much technological advancement is made, progress can never bring about spiritual peace, because it lacks the basis for that peace. And the advances of a higher standard of living can never bring fulfillment to a life devoid of peace.

The scientific concept of the world has replaced the old mythical ones and the old teachings are no longer accepted as naively as before. Science has helped us overcome certain anxieties about understanding and living in the world, which used to be a main focus of religion. Consequently, the ground for belief in a god's existence has become weaker, and religious truths have often come to be treated as pagan superstitions. There is no longer a place for the "soothing" religions that hope to solve problems by mysterious, magical powers, when these same matters are gradually being resolved by natural science. Therefore, if the continued existence of a religion is to be justified, then that religion will have to concern itself with overcoming those anxieties that cannot be assuaged by scientific advances, and with helping us find a new basis for a sense of direction in our lives. What it will have to do is deal with the pursuit of peace in the purest sense.

This civilization is a crazy one, galloping onward like a wild horse. It is becoming increasingly urgent to establish true religion alongside this civilization based on science and technology, to enable us to regain spiritual peace. We must pursue in a practical and serious way a religion incorporating peace in the truest sense—a peace that cannot be achieved by the development of scientific technology but is not incompatible with it.

Goethe writes in *Faust* to the effect that as long as man marches on, he is torn between choices. Is that to be the fate of humanity? Or is it possible for us to discover a path whereby we may progress while being at peace, or, being at total peace, a path whereby we may make progress?

Self Settling on Itself

Dissatisfied with the inability of technology to fulfill their lives, Westerners have come to show a deep concern for the East, straining to look into its essence and exploring Buddhism, which reveals a remarkable and unique characteristic among religions: Buddhism does not raise the question of god. Consequently, for a time Christian-influenced scholars even denied it was a religion. However, it is nonsense to decide whether or not a teaching is a religion by the presence or absence of the concept of god. If we decide that something qualifies as a religion only on that basis, then religion must have disappeared when the mythological worldview came to be replaced by the worldview of natural science. The presence or absence of a god concept is not what is most fundamental, since religion must be that which teaches humanity what is most important in life and offers genuine spiritual peace. In this most fundamental sense, Buddhism is pure religion.

Since Buddhism is a religion that does not raise the question of god, what is its basis for peace of mind? In contrast to a posture of bowing down before the God of Christianity or some god of another religion, the fundamental posture of Buddhism is the true self settling on the true self. This fundamental posture is to settle upon our undeniable, immovable self without being dragged about by our unstable thoughts. This attitude is unchanged from that of the founder of Buddhism, Shakyamuni Buddha.

In the *Suttanipata,* which is said to be the oldest Buddhist scripture, the Buddha says, "Live in the world relying on the self alone as a foundation, be freed from all things, depending on no thing." In the *Dhammapada* he says, "The foundation of self is only self," and in the Mahaparinirvana Sutra ("The Sutra of the Great Passing," the Buddha's last days) is the famous phrase, "Take refuge in self, take refuge in dharma [truth], take refuge in nothing else." These passages from the earliest scriptures reflect the basic attitude of Shakyamuni himself. However, with even the slightest misunderstanding of this attitude there is the danger of a very foolish civilization being created. One mistake, and today's scientific civilization becomes a kind of madness. If you take one distinctive feature of human nature and develop it as if it were the whole self without seeing the truth of human life, the result is likely to be insane.

Just as modern civilization exerts itself foolishly, ignoring the truth of human life, so immediately after the Buddha's death practitioners with a small-minded attitude developed a mistaken trend. They misinterpreted the spirit of the Buddha's words "self settling on itself, seeking nothing else" to mean that one should become fixed on death. They thought that by extinguishing outwardly directed desires they could arrive at a quiet nirvana. Consequently, their samadhi of self settling on itself came to mean an escape into a life devoid of activity except for a focus on death. It goes without saying that therein the truth of human life was lost.

The misconception that Buddhism is isolationist and pessimistic can be attributed to this misinterpretation. Still, if one is not careful, the samadhi of self settling on itself can take on a retrogressive tendency to indulge in escapism. This point must always be borne in mind as we uncover Buddhist samadhi, or zazen.

In contrast to isolationism or escapism, practitioners with a broader attitude developed a living samadhi. *Samadhi* refers to self settling on true and immovable self, but "immovable" should not be interpreted to mean functionless or fixed in an inactive state. Since this universal self is life and life is activity, life completely unhindered by anything manifests as pure activity. This is immovable, unshakable life.

Within the manifestation of pure life, practitioners found where the whole self can settle, and this led to the development of Mahayana Buddhism. In brief, self settling on itself does not mean to be dragged around by desirous thoughts nor, on the other hand, does it mean to become lifeless, with vitality wasting away. Life must function as activity that manifests life as life. And through this kind of activity an immeasurable and alive world will open before us.

In order that our discussion not remain abstract, let us turn back to the concrete everyday world. For instance, why do we work? We could say we work in order to eat, or to better our standard of living, or to become famous. However, all of these responses originate out of our own personal thoughts and desires and not from the life force itself.

The lily blooming in the field—why does it bloom? It does not bloom for any particular purpose; it blooms solely because it has been given life. "Consider the lilies of the field, how they grow; they toil not, neither do they spin. And yet I say unto you, that even Solomon in all his glory was not arrayed like one of these" (Matthew 6:28–29). Here the glory of life simply appears. In the same way, the violet blooms as a violet, and the rose expresses its life as a rose. The flowers blooming in the field do not feel with pride that they should win first prize in a beauty contest; they do not feel that they are in competition with other flowers. The violet does not develop an inferiority complex, thinking, "The roses are big and beautiful, but a little violet like myself is useless." It doesn't say with greed and impatience, "I've got to become more efficient." It simply manifests its own life force with all its might.

Of course, if a violet plant cannot produce even a small violet, it is unable to make seeds and continue its line. Nevertheless, when it blooms it does so for no personal purpose. Just bringing forth flowers is its life. There is a passage in the Lotus Sutra that reads, "All things are the truth in themselves." In Zen, a similar expression is, "A willow is green, a flower is red." In short, Buddhism as a religious teaching means manifesting the world of life in which a violet blooms as a violet and a rose as a rose.

In the Amitayus Sutra of the Pure Land teachings, paradise is described in this way: "Blue things are blue, red things are red... This is the Pure Land [paradise]." This point demands our close attention. Without thinking carefully about it, we imagine how wonderful it would be if blue things could become red, or that poor people would be happy if only they could become rich.

Obviously, I don't in any way mean to imply that it is bad for poor people to become rich. But happiness does not invariably come with wealth, nor unhappiness with poverty. If you fix it in your mind that the materially rich are happy and poor people are unhappy, then when you are poor, you will surely be unhappy. It's a mistake to hold on to such a view. For those who think this way, no matter now much money they have, the time will come when it will be useless. At death, such people will fall into the depths of misery.

There is no fixed line above which we can definitively assert that a person is rich, while below it everyone is poor. Since rich and poor are nothing but relative comparisons, when we let go of the comparison we will always be able to settle just as our universal self.

Even though some people may call me poor or rich, they are simply comparing me with someone else and trying to put a label on me, so it has nothing to do with the reality of who I am. Returning to the reality of my life just as myself—just manifesting this life—is the meaning of the saying that blue things are blue and red things are red. This is the pure land.

In other words, without being tossed about by personal feelings and ideas, just returning to the life of my true self, without envying or being arrogant toward those around me, neither being self-deprecating nor competing with others, yet on the other hand not falling into the trap of laziness, negligence, or carelessness—just manifesting that life of my self with all the vigor I have—here is where the glory of life comes forth and where the light of buddha shines.[53] Religious light shines where we manifest our own life.

In Buddhism, the world that unfolds as true self settling on true self is not a world where the strong devour the weak or where people struggle for mere survival, nor is it a world of escapism or seclusion where one has forgotten to bring forth the flower of one's life. It is a world that opens the flower of self alone; it is a world that opens the present alone. Buddhist samadhi—that is, zazen—is the foundation for the manifestation of this life.

Interdependence and the Middle Way

To look more deeply into the Buddhist notion of life, we have to take up the teachings of interdependence and the Middle Way. Buddhist teachings explain self as life, and they explain the vivid world self lives in as interdependence, or the Middle Way.[54] To digest the zazen of the true self settling on itself as Buddhism, we have to step back and look at these teachings.

The early scriptures known as the *Agamas,* or the *Nikayas,* say "Truly seeing the aggregation of the world, the view of nonexistence does not arise. Truly seeing the nonsubstantiality of the world, the view of existence does not arise. The view that all things exist is one extreme; the view that nothing exists is the other extreme. Being apart from these two extremes, the Tathagata teaches the dharma of the Middle Way: because this exists, that exists; because this arises, that arises."[55]

The entire teaching of interdependence and the Middle Way is explained in this one quotation. Moreover, what is expressed here is the very essence of the spirit that developed as Mahayana Buddhism. Although the language of this passage is so simple it is not easily understood, we can try to get a sense of it in terms of everyday life.

The scripture says of interdependence "Because this exists, that exists, because this arises, that arises." But what does this mean? It means that all concrete entities occur in accordance with various conditions, that they always happen based on conditions and never apart from or separate from such factors, and that all abstract entities have meaning because of their mutual relations. Accordingly, what is being said here is that there are no independent substantial entities—that is, no things exist by themselves.

Usually we think of our "self" as an individual independent substance, an enduring existence. But if we think about it carefully, this is by no means the case. I have an album of photographs taken of me every few years from infancy on. When I look at it these days I am filled with an utterly strange feeling. It so clearly shows the changes I have gone through while gradually advancing in age. How my face and figure have changed with the years! I can only wonder at the marvel of creation. Within this constant change, what endures? The birthmark under my eye, the peculiar slope of my head—only these meaningless facts remain. And if it is true that I am only what endures through time, then this birthmark and this oddly shaped head are what I truly am. I cannot help but wonder whether these pictures are all of the same *I* or not.

Not only the appearance of the body, but the inside as well, is gradually being regenerated and transformed; so what does not appear in photographs is also undergoing change.

Moreover, the content of my thoughts, which I refer to as *I,* has also been radically changing, from infancy to childhood, adolescence, maturity, and now in old age. Not just that—even this present *I* is an unceasing stream of consciousness. Yet, taken momentarily at a given time, we grasp the stream of consciousness as a fixed thing and call it *I.*

We are as selves quite like the flame of a candle. As wax melts near a lit wick and burns it emits light near the tip of the candle that appears as a more-or-less fixed shape. It is this seemingly unchanging shape that we refer to as flame. What we call *I* is similar to the flame. Although both body and mind are an unceasing flow, since they preserve what seems to be a constant form we refer to them as *I.* Actually there is no *I* existing as some substantial thing; there is only the ceaseless flow. This is true not only of me, it is true of all things. In Buddhism, this truth is expressed as *shogyō mujō,* the first undeniable reality, that all things are flowing and changing, and *shohō muga,* the third undeniable reality, that all things are insubstantial.

Impermanence is ungraspable, but this never implies nonexistence. We live within the flow of impermanence, maintaining a temporary form similar to an eddy in the flow of a river. Though the water is always flowing, the eddy, like the flame of the candle, arises out of various conditions as a form that seems to be fixed. That there is this seemingly fixed form that is based on various conditions is interdependence. In the case of the flame, it is the interdependence of such things as the wax, the temperature, and the air; in the case of the eddy, it is the volume and speed of the current, the topography, and so forth, that form the conditions of its existence.

Not only such things as eddies and flames, but indeed everything in the universe can be considered in a similar way. For example, we who live in the age of natural science can easily appreciate that no matter how solid a thing may appear, it is not really different from the flame or the eddy—its apparent solidity is merely a question of degree.

Returning to the question of *self,* I, too, am an interdependent existence that is impermanent and at the same time takes a particular form. Buddhism teaches that our attachment to our self as though it were a substantial being is the source of our greed, anger, suffering, and strife. It is crucial that we reflect thoroughly on the fact that our self does not have a substantial existence; rather it has an interdependent existence.

What is it that we think of as our *self?* Physically, this self originates in the union of sperm and egg and is brought to its present form through the combination of such factors as temperature, moisture, nutrition, and the like. And what is it that makes up our mental life or personality? Here again, I have not chosen this self, but have simply received life in my mother's womb unconsciously, or ignorantly.[56] I received the foundation of my personality plus innumerable hereditary elements from my parents. Without realizing it, I was educated according to my particular society, era, and family, and I internalized my experiences within this environment. In this way, through the combination of an accidental set of factors, the views I now hold have been formed.

So our *self* is a random collection of elements and circumstances and not some sort of lump, as it is usually understood. This self may become deluded, but as it is not a fixed entity, this delusion also breaks apart. The true reality of life is expressed in the Buddha's twelvefold chain of interdependence, insight into which is said to have been the source of his enlightenment.[57] This self as an interdependent being is simply a collection of elements, but insofar as it possesses some form as a particular collection it is not nonexistent. This is the point of the scriptural passage from the Nikayas quoted earlier: "Truly seeing the aggregation of the world, the view of nonexistence does not arise."

But, if this present self is not nonexistent, can we say that it is a constant entity? No; rather, it is breaking apart and changing into a new form moment after moment. This is the meaning of "Truly seeing the nonsubstantiality of the world, the view of existence does not arise."

Consequently, the Buddha said, "Being apart from these two extremes [the views based on existence or nonexistence], the Tathagata—the Enlightened One—teaches the dharma of the Middle Way." This means that our very own life cannot be grasped as an existing lump, nor as nonexistence. The Middle Way is nothing other than seeing interdependence as it is, moment by moment; it is seeing our life as it is, without being caught up in our thoughts.

Therefore, the Middle Way in Buddhism does not mean taking some in-between position that has been conjured up in our heads, nor acting in a compromising way. Rather, despite the fact that we latch on to our ideas of being or nonbeing, taking the Middle Way means to demolish all concepts set up in our minds and, without fixing on reality as any particular thing, to open the hand of thought, allowing life to be life.

Delusion and Zazen

The zazen taught in Zen Buddhism is the actualization of the Middle Way that is at the very quick of life; it is life as life—that is, life as interdependence. Zazen enables life to be life by letting it be.

One might well ask: Whether we exert ourselves or not, aren't we always living life as it is? Isn't it nonsense to speak of living apart from life? This is indeed so, and it is the basis of the Buddhist teaching that all beings have buddha nature. That is, actualizing life is our very nature.

Nevertheless, it is also true that we aren't always living fully, we aren't always actualizing our life. This is because unlike the flowers in the fields, human beings bear the burden of thought. Thought has a dual nature: thought springs from life, and yet it has the ability to think of things totally ungrounded and detached from the fact of life. This is delusion and it leads to some strange consequences.

A politician says to herself, "I've got to whip Tanaka in the election," and her heart races—though she is alone in her room talking to herself and not in the midst of any competition. A man goads himself deliriously with thoughts of "I'm going to get my hands on that mine and make myself a fortune," though he is not within reach of it and there is no price tag hanging from pieces of the ore.

Being detached by our thoughts from reality, we fabricate seemingly substantial and accumulable entities such as money, position, or power right in the middle of this insubstantial world. This is the view of existence. In order to possess these things, we become greedy and deceitful, hating and injuring each other, or else we hold on to feelings of inferiority that develop into neuroses in the course of our struggle. Delusion is this very view of myself as an independent substantial entity.

Even though this world of interdependence is not substantial, provisionally it has a certain order. Yet we ignore that order—taking up the view of nonexistence—and pursue selfish desires, throwing all our energy into killing one another and destroying the things around us, living for the moment and in the end short-circuiting our lives.

In other words our thought, whether through the view of existence or of nonexistence, becomes the basis for the distortions of our lives that prevent life from manifesting in a straightforward way as it truly is. In Buddhism, thought as the foundation of these views of existence and nonexistence is referred to as ego-attachment. Ego-attachment is our clinging to "substance" and calling it *I*, which in our ignorance we have falsely constructed in the constantly shifting world of interdependence.

In other words, egocentricity lies at the basis of whatever we see or do. It tags along with us. Being dragged around by egocentric thought, our life cannot manifest directly and winds up pushed out of shape and disabled. This being dragged about by egocentric thought has been committed by humankind since its beginning. Adam and Eve truly put us in a mess.[58]

I saw a fascinating cartoon in a newspaper some years ago. Adam was trying with all his might to vomit up something he had eaten. Eve was standing beside him with a worried expression, saying, "Adam, hasn't that apple you ate come out yet?" If only humanity could once and for all vomit up that indigestible green apple of ego-attachment. In a way, egocentric thought is a little like "original sin." In Buddhism, true zazen is, in a sense, the posture of vomiting up that apple. But when did we eat the apple? It was by no means in some remote mythical past. Here we are, merely interdependent existences, a collection of such accidental factors as heredity, the overall current of the times, and the social context in which we find ourselves. Without any good reason, moved by ignorance, we pompously stick a label onto this aggregation, calling it *I*. We firmly believe that this is our self, and we cling to ego as though it simply existed in the natural order of things. Actually, outside of the power of ignorance, which causes attachment to the ego-self in each moment, where is that apple we ate? That apple is precisely what we are eating again and again in our attachment to ourselves.

Yet to vomit up this apple is no easy matter. Even if we understand that there is no reason to stick the label of "self" onto an aggregation of various coincidental factors and to get attached to this label, and if moreover we understand that this attachment to ego is the source of various evils, delusions, and sufferings, and therefore ought to be vomited up—even if we understand all this, we still cannot vomit up the apple. For our ego-attachment does not occur merely on the surface of consciousness; we are eating that apple prior to our conscious awareness—that is, in the depths of our subconscious. Indeed, it may well be that in our very desire to throw up the apple, the poison of the apple is at work. At this point, human intellect serves no purpose at all, for it is precisely *using our head* that is being called into question.

The practice of zazen is a unique development for dismantling this lump of ignorant ego-attachment. Zazen is the posture that throws away this "self" composed of ignorance and no longer entertains the thoughts of ego-attachment that push up from within. As for the actual posture of zazen, it is just the opposite of Rodin's *The Thinker,* whose back, waist, legs, arms, and even fingers and toes are all bent (recall figure 10, on page 46). Calling such a form *The Thinker* sounds nice, but actually it is a posture given over to fabrication, to peering into an internal hell. The zazen posture is the opposite of *The Thinker*'s: everything is straight.

In the zazen posture we are able to calm down, and our mental excitability diminishes. It is by nature a posture in which it is impossible to think continuously about the same thing, and the fictions we set up in our heads dissolve. Therefore, when doing zazen we just sit, letting go of everything that comes up. All that has been learned is given back to learning, all that is memorized is given back to memory, all that has been thought is given back to thought. To let go of everything—that is the posture of zazen.

When we are doing zazen, does this mean that thoughts no longer arise and that our heads become empty? No, of course not. As long as we are alive it is only natural that various thoughts arise, even when we are doing zazen. What is crucial is to let them come and go of themselves without pursuing them or driving them out. For example, a thought comes up: if we follow it, then we are thinking and no longer sitting zazen, even though we are in the zazen posture. In zazen, it is important not to chase after thoughts. On the other hand, when a thought comes up, should we try to wipe it out? If we do, then we end up thinking that we have to try to wipe out that thought. Rather, when doing zazen, we commit everything to the posture, without chasing after or chasing out thoughts. In the same way, when we take the zazen posture, if we doze off we are napping and not doing zazen. Just as doing zazen is not thinking while sitting, neither is it napping or dozing off while sitting. Therefore, full of vigor, we just aim at the correct zazen posture with our flesh and bones. Just practicing this is doing zazen.

Moreover, it is of utmost importance here not to indulge in self-observation. Self-observation, or observing the effect of our zazen, such as being calmer or more agitated, not only misses the mark, but the moment we do so, we impair zazen and go off the track. Zazen has nothing to do with thinking about results. It is essential just to aim at the posture of zazen without trying to observe its effects.

You may feel that being unable to observe the effect of your zazen will lead to tremendous dissatisfaction. It is only natural to feel this, for zazen throws out our petty thoughts that seek satisfaction and manifests life purely as life. The feeling that something is lacking is no more than our petty thoughts of being unfulfilled. Sawaki Roshi used to say, "There is no reason to expect the reality of immeasurable and unbounded life to satisfy your puny little thoughts."

Only when we let go of all such ideas will our life find peace in the purity of full life, because it is just these dissatisfied thoughts and our being tangled in ideas of existence or nonexistence that throw our lives into anxiety and drag us into suffering, fighting, hopelessness, and despair. It is through the posture of letting go of these thoughts that we are able to discover the absolute peace of life.

Nevertheless, this peace is not the cessation or extinction of life; it is not seclusion or escapism. Far from it. Living in peace is the unfettered realization of life as life and is not at all off in the clouds. Rather, all reality, undisturbed by thought, is reflected as it interdependently appears and disappears. Genuine peace is like a clear mirror that simply reflects all images as they are, without anything sticking to it.

Zazen is itself practicing the Middle Way with our own bodies. This Middle Way is itself true life. This can be seen in our daily lives as well. For example when we are driving a car, if we are tense, or absorbed in our thoughts, our life becomes totally confused and we cannot manifest it as it is. Our driving becomes highly dangerous. At the same time, it is hazardous to drive when sleepy or drunk, which also blinds us. We can drive safely only when we are relaxed and at the same time wide awake.

Zazen is the posture through which our life force manifests itself most naturally and purely.

SEVEN

Living Wide Awake

Zazen as Religion

Behind zazen there is the religion of Buddhism, and behind that, our own lives. Consequently, the true or genuine zazen found in Buddhist scriptures was never intended as a means of disciplining the mind or of becoming physically healthier. Our ideas about a mind to be trained or a body to be made healthy are expressions of the view of existence, which presupposes that there are things that can be accumulated. The wish to train and discipline our minds and bodies is nothing but our own egoistic desire. For zazen to function as religion, it is of primary concern to give up this ego-centered way of thinking that clings to body and mind.

Zazen may or may not be called a religion, depending on how the word is defined. In most cases, the word "religion" is used to mean a sect or creed or doctrine; however, zazen is in no sense a doctrine or creed, nor should it be.

109

Religion has long been concerned with people's relationship to an authority above them. People come under a suggestive spell through the words of that authority and proceed to call the complete submission to that authority religion. However, Zen is not a religion in this sense, either.

Zen Buddhism does not recognize any authority outside of the true self. This is the traditional way passed down since Shakyamuni, who told his disciples, as I said earlier, "Take refuge in self, take refuge in dharma, do not take refuge in anything else." Just before the Buddha died, his attendant Ananda wanted to call together his many disciples, but he wouldn't allow it. He said, "People do not belong to me." He simply lived out his own life, refusing to become the object of worship of his disciples and followers. This was his basic attitude toward life. Zen Buddhism has inherited Shakyamuni's basic life attitude, which is to just live out the life of the universal self. We simply actualize within the self the most refined attitude toward life. If religion means the teaching about the most refined attitude toward life, then Buddhism is certainly pure religion, since to live out the life of the self does not mean the self-intoxication of some egocentric self. On the contrary, this is the attitude of discovering the life within the self that is connected to all things. It means aiming at manifesting the life of each and every encounter, and seeing all of these encounters as our own life. This life attitude is referred to in Buddhism as compassion. A person unable to find compassion toward others cannot be called a person of zazen who has awakened to the reality of the life of the whole self.

In the Bible it is written: "Thy will be done" (Matthew 6:10); "Whether you eat or drink, or whatever you do, do all to the glory of God" (I Corinthians 10:31); and "We love Him [God] because He loved us first.... He who loves God must also love his brother" (John 4:19, 21). This basic Christian attitude toward the religious life is also the basic Buddhist attitude.

In Buddhism as religion, zazen—in which we let go of all these human thoughts and feelings—is the foundation of our lives. It is zazen that protects, guides, and gives strength to our daily actions, as well as to our lives as a whole, and in turn to the society in which we live. Therefore, we can say that zazen is for the Buddhist much as God is for the Christian. Psalms 46:10 says, "Be still, and know that I am God." Zazen certainly actualizes this in the purest way. In Luke 17:20–21 there is, "The kingdom of God comes not with observation: Neither shall they say, Lo here! or Lo there! For, behold, the kingdom of God is within you" (see also Matthew 12:18, Acts 17:27–28, Romans 14:17, I Corinthians 2:9). In zazen we can see directly this kingdom within us. In Matthew 6:5–7 is written:

> And when you pray, do not be as the hypocrites are: for they love to pray standing in the synagogues and at the street corners to be seen by other people. I assure you, they have been paid in full. But, you, when you pray, enter your inner room, and with your door closed, pray to your Father who is there in the secret place, and your Father who sees in secret will reward you. When you pray, do not repeat as the pagans do.
>
> There is no purer way of expressing this attitude toward prayer than zazen. "My Father, if it be possible, let this cup pass from me; however, not as I will, but as you will" (Matthew 26:39).

"God be merciful to me a sinner" (Luke 18:13). "Our Father who is in heaven, your name be kept holy. Your kingdom come, your will be done on earth as in heaven" (Matthew 6:9–10).

The essence of this pure prayer is all included in the prayer that takes the form of zazen. How can we approach truth or, to a Christian, God with bodies that are full of confusion and evil? For that, zazen must have vow and repentance as a backing. To express this from the opposite side, zazen as true religion must include vow and repentance.

Vow and Repentance

Doing zazen is letting go of clinging to human thought, and this means letting go, or throwing out, human arrogance. With that we become, as the Bible says, "as God wills," and then "the works of God will be manifest" (John 9:3).

What this means becomes clear when we compare zazen with a life based on thought. We are constantly discriminating and dividing everything into this and that, based on our thinking. To throw out sequential thinking, not tying one phenomenon to another, is to be prior to thought. It is to be before the separation of things into *this* and *that*. When we are practicing zazen we exist before separating this moment from eternity, or subject from object. This may sound merely theoretical, but for a practitioner of zazen, it is not the result of reasoning; rather, zazen enables one to experience this directly.

Although zazen is prior to the separation of all things, this is not to say that in zazen we lose consciousness; since life is being vigorously manifested, all things are reflected, and self here-and-now is not lost. But what does it mean to say that in zazen, although everything is before division or discrimination, there is no loss of self here and now? It means that self here and now is eternity, the whole earth, all sentient beings.

This is a remarkable thing. I'm not saying it is logically so, rather that since the reality of zazen is such, we are concretely enabled to directly experience through zazen the self in which this moment is one with eternity.

Living by zazen as religion is found in our functioning day to day as a *person,* a role that is itself the personified union of this moment and eternity. Living every day by surrendering to zazen, being protected and guided by zazen, means to live having a direction—that is, living without being pulled around by the thoughts and emotions rampaging inside us. This means to live aiming at enacting the unity of the present and the eternal.

Taking as reality what precedes division, we will not conjure up objects of desire, opponents, competitors, and so on. As long as we are walking in this direction we will not labor under the burdens of greed, impatience, and envy; we will not go around cheating, deceiving, wounding, and killing one another. Rather, as true self that is only true self, we possess absolute peace within us. At the same time, since we aim at manifesting the vigorous self that is here and now, and is simultaneously one with eternity, we need to make unceasing effort.

Our life as a person lies precisely where we live in peace while progressing. Dōgen Zenji refers to this as the identity of practice and enlightenment. This is without a doubt the structure of the actualization of life.

In "Only Buddha Together with Buddha" *(Shōbōgenzō: Yuibutsu-yobutsu),* Dōgen Zenji writes, "The activity of buddha is carried on together with the whole earth and all living beings; if it is not activity that is one with all things, it is not buddha activity." People who practice true zazen can confirm as actual experience what Dōgen Zenji is pointing out in this passage as the foundation of daily life. Acting in accordance with the entire earth and with all beings is zazen practitioners' whole life direction, and simultaneously it is their direction right here and now. In Buddhism, this life direction is referred to as vow.

I have spoken of zazen as religion and quoted several passages from the Bible; however, I should point out that living by vow is quite different from the religious life of the Christian, for in Buddhism there is no notion of sacrifice. What the Christian does in the spirit of sacrifice, the Buddhist does on the basis of vow. The spirit of sacrifice arises from first separating *I* and *thou,* and then *I* is given over to the service of *thou.* But Buddhism looks at life prior to the division of *I* and *thou.*

The encounter between *I* and *thou* in Buddhism is like that between a mother and her child. The mother takes care of her child, but in doing so, she is not sacrificing herself; on the contrary, with a nurturing love she looks after the child as her own life. In the Lotus Sutra the Buddha says, "The three worlds are my possessions, and all sentient beings therein are my children." This is the fundamental spirit of Buddhism, and the source of this spirit is nothing other than settling in the zazen that precedes all distinctions.

In other words, for the person who sits zazen, vow is nothing other than the practitioner's own life. We take all encounters— with things, situations, people, society—as nothing but our own life, and we act with a spirit of looking after everything as our own life. Therefore, like the mother's caring for her child, we aim to function unconditionally and tirelessly and, moreover, to do so without expecting any reward.

It is not to profit personally or to become famous that we take good care of things, devote ourselves to our work, love those whom we encounter, or demonstrate our concern for social problems. When I take care of my own life, I take care of the world as my own life. I do this moment by moment, and in each situation I enable the flower of my life to bloom, working solely that the light of buddha may shine.

In this sense, the activity of buddha being carried on together with the whole earth and all living beings is the aim of zazen practitioners' daily life as well as the aim or vow of our overall life. It is through zazen that we make this vow our own.

Even though in our zazen our activity is carried on together with the whole earth and all beings, there is no way we can carry out perfect action like a buddha. To think that we have achieved perfect action is simply to be arrogant. For thinking in such a way is, after all, nothing more than our own human judgment. In our zazen, precisely because we have taken such a vow, we cannot help but repent of our inability to fulfill it.

Will the matter be settled simply by feeling bad about our inadequacy? No, faced with the absolute nature of reality, this will not do. A pickpocket might confess to his boss, "I'm sorry, I blew it." A soldier might confess at his court-martial, "I'm sorry I wasn't brave enough to kill the enemy." In other words, our thought of having done something bad is only based on some conventional, changing standard or idea. Before absolutely real reality, it is totally meaningless.

To truly repent does not mean offering an apology; rather, repenting requires facing life straight on, and letting the light of absolute reality illuminate us. What does it mean to be illuminated by absolute reality? The Samantabhadra Bodhisattva Dhyana Sutra says, "If you wish to repent, sit zazen and contemplate the true nature of all things." In other words, it is in doing zazen that true repentance is actualized.

We who practice zazen hold this vow, and function with it as our life direction, while at the same time we just keep returning to zazen repenting at being unable to carry out that vow. This is what constitutes the religious life of the Buddhist practitioner: living by vow and repentance, and being watched over, protected, and given strength by zazen. Where there is no vow, we lose sight of progress; where there is no repentance, we lose the way. Vow gives us courage; repentance crushes our arrogance. This is the posture of a vivid, alive religious life.

The Bodhisattva Vow

A person who discovers the direction of his life in zazen, who vows and at the same time lives by repentance through zazen, is called a bodhisattva.[59] This means that a bodhisattva is an ordinary person who has found her life direction in buddha, in practicing the way of life of a buddha. You are a bodhisattva, I am a bodhisattva. There are illustrious bodhisattvas like Kannon (Skt. Avalokiteshvara) and Monju (Skt. Manjushri), who embody compassion and wisdom, but we have to have confidence that we, too, are bodhisattvas. Even as ordinary human beings, when we live by vow the meaning of our lives totally changes.

A bodhisattva living by vow is distinguished from a person living by the continuation of his karma. There is no need to deprecate ourselves thinking that, since we are ordinary human beings, we aren't qualified to be bodhisattvas. Precisely because we are ordinary human beings, we possess this earthly flesh; yet, since we aim in the direction of buddha in zazen, we can make our effort in peace.

Most people live by their desires or karma. They go through their lives dragged around by desires and hindered by the consequences of previous harmful actions. In Japanese that kind of life is called *gosshō no bompu*. *Gosshō* are the obstructions to practicing the Way caused by our evil actions in the past. *Bompu* simply means ordinary human being—that is, one who lives by karma. Our actions are dictated by our karma: we are born into this world with our desires and may live our whole lives just reacting or responding to them.

In contrast to that is the way of life of a bodhisattva who lives by vow *(ganshō no bosatsu)*. The life that flows through each of us and through everything around us is actually all connected. To say that, of course, means that who I really am cannot be separated from all the things that surround me. Or, to put it another way, all sentient beings have their existence and live within my life. This includes even the fate of all humankind—that, too, lies within me. Therefore, my direction becomes just how humanity might truly live out its life. In other words, it is the motivation for living that is different for a bodhisattva. Ordinary people live thinking only about their own personal, narrow circumstances connected with their desires. In contrast to that a bodhisattva, though undeniably still an ordinary human being like everyone else, lives aiming at the well-being of everyone, as the direction of his or her own life. For us as bodhisattvas all aspects of life, including the fate of humanity itself, live within us. It is with this in mind that we work to discover and manifest the most vital and alive posture we can find for living out our life.

In our day-to-day lives it is often hard to know what course of action best expresses our bodhisattva vow, because circumstances pull us in contradictory directions. Going one way seems right and so does going in the opposite direction. How do you choose between competing "goods"? This is a very difficult problem. Most religious systems have a set of absolutes handed down by their God that tell you what is right or wrong. Buddhism has no absolute authority laying down the law. Instead, you yourself take up the way of a bodhisattva, living by vow and aiming at buddha. Because this is such an important issue and it always turns on the concrete details of the situation, I want to tell you a story at some length. It comes from Dōgen Zenji's *Regulations for Eihei Monastery (Eihei Shingi)*, in the section entitled "Regulations for the Officers" *(Chiji Shingi)*.

Guixing, a Zen master in Shexuan, China, was noted for his severity in training his disciples and for simplicity and frugality in his own daily affairs. He was highly respected by the monks who practiced under him.

When Zen masters Fayuan of Shuzhou and Yihuai of Tianyi were young practitioners, they traveled a long way with some other young monks just to train under Guixing. It was the dead of winter when they arrived, but Guixing only shouted at them and told them to go away. On top of that, he threw water on them to get them to leave. Their robes were completely drenched. Everyone else left angrily, but Fayuan and Yihuai simply straightened their robes and sat zazen. Guixing shouted at them again. "Haven't you guys gone yet?

Get the hell out of here or I'll beat you up!"

People who are searching for the Way can't be called true seekers if they're going to pick up and pack their bags just because they get a little water thrown on them. If you're serious in your searching and intention to become someone's disciple, you have to be prepared to take whatever comes. To practice Buddhism means to encounter the reality of life. Before I became a monk, I studied philosophy and Christianity, and lived in a world of ideas. To become a monk, however, meant I had to meet the reality of my life headon, whatever it was, without trying to escape. When I became a monk, we were up every morning at 4 A.M. for zazen, then we chanted sutras, ate breakfast, and worked outside until dark. In the evening we sat zazen for two more hours. I was always cold at night, so I could never get to sleep. When four o'clock rolled around and we had to get up, there I'd be, shaking from the cold.

I kept feeling this was the first time in my life that I was confronted with the reality of life, and that it was essential for me not to look for a way out. There is a Buddhist expression, "Don't love dragons like Sekkō." There was a man called Sekkō who loved dragons. Sculptures, paintings, figurines, ornaments—his whole house was filled with dragons in one form or another. Well, one day a real dragon happened to hear about Sekkō and figured that since he loved dragons so much, surely he would be delighted to meet a real one. But when the dragon stuck his head through the window of Sekkō's room, Sekkō expired on the spot!

Sekkō is a symbol for preferring imitation to the real thing. A person who tells everyone how important practice is and then gives up soon after he starts because it's too hard to take is like a person who just likes sculpted dragons. When you meet a real "dragon" you should be filled with joy and resolve to wrestle with it.

Fayuan approached Guixing. "We've had to walk more than a thousand miles to get here. Don't think that you can drive us away by beating us or by splashing a little water on us."

The power of life that is buried deep inside you will never rise up until you have become convinced that you're walking the only path open for you. As weak-kneed as I was in those days, somehow I became a monk and managed to make it through the war and its aftermath despite the chaotic circumstances of that time. I was able to get through it all because I was convinced that there was no other way of life for me. There is no way you could have gotten through those days thinking that if this didn't work out you could always find something else to do. This is something we should always be sure of—that is, always walking the path that leaves no room for waffling. Only then will the power arise within you that will enable you to say, "Don't think you can drive us away by beating us or by splashing a little water on us."

It's nothing to have a little water dumped over your head, but just to sit facing a wall with the attitude that it's nothing at all can be incredibly difficult. Yet, once you sit with the conviction that zazen is the ultimate activity and perform that activity with the sense of it being nothing at all, then just that becomes ultimate activity.

Guixing laughed. "All right, you two may stay and practice zazen here."

Only when they proved that they were in earnest about walking the way of ultimate reality were they allowed to stay on and practice.

Shortly after, Fayuan was asked to serve as tenzo [head cook]. The monks in the monastery were suffering under the severity of the discipline. Then it happened that Guixing left the monastery for a day.

So, after a short time, Fayuan became the tenzo of the monastery. Now, this Guixing really went to extremes with his severity, and the monks, having nothing substantial to eat, were suffering miserably.

Fayuan stole the key to the storage room and took out enough flour for noodles to make a feast for all the monks.

Here's an interesting point about Dōgen Zenji. Many people who write about Dōgen create the impression that he was all purity and innocence and would never think of stealing. Yet here he is praising Fayuan's theft of flour.

Everyone is chafing under the harness of Guixing's discipline—they're all suffering from malnutrition. But Fayuan knows that there is plenty of flour in the storage room, so he sneaks into the room, hauls out a load of flour, and proceeds to put together a meal to put the monks back on their feet.

This was all very admirable of him to do—as long as he remained fully aware of what the probable consequences would be, a beating by the abbot. To be willing to put yourself out for everyone—that's the attitude of a bodhisattva. All our actions should be taken with the spirit of giving life to the overall situation surrounding us. And despite thinking in those terms, if you make a mistake, then you have to be willing to pay the price. It's no good shrinking from the hell you might have to pay for the deed. Dōgen makes a point of praising Fayuan, saying, "We should learn particularly from Fayuan's attitude. The attitude he showed toward his practice is extremely rare—his manner of doings things is something that should be considered carefully." This is the kind of man Dōgen was and it reflects the underlying tone of the entire "Regulations for the Officers."

Suddenly, Guixing returned.

Fayuan has been working on this fantastic meal, and just as it's being put on the table and everyone's gathered around, who should be there sitting down ready to eat along with everyone else but Guixing!

> *After the meal Guixing sat outside the hall and called for the tenzo. Fayuan came and Guixing asked him, "Did you steal flour from the storage room for that meal?"*

You can be sure he was hopping mad, since he'd probably been saving that flour for some time.

> *Fayuan took no time in replying. "Yes, I did. Punish me as you will."*

"Well, whatever it cost, get out, go sell your robes and bowl, and pay for it! And after that, you'll get thirty strokes and a boot out of here!"

Guixing really let him have it with both barrels, not only making him pay for it, but throwing him out and promising to beat him besides.

Fayuan left the temple and found a place to stay in the nearby town. As the lodging was owned by the temple, he had a brother disciple go to the temple for him to ask the abbot's permission to stay there. But Guixing refused.

In those days in China, temples often had guest houses located nearby. Fayuan probably figured Guixing would allow him to stay there since it wasn't on the temple grounds proper, but Guixing turned him down flat.

Fayuan then asked through his friend simply to be allowed to return to live in the main hall and follow along in practice with all of the other monks, completely forfeiting his former position in the temple. Again Guixing refused. One day, when Guixing happened to leave the temple again on business, he saw Fayuan standing in front of one of the temple's lodging places. "So this is where you've been staying. You know, this is temple property. How many days have you been here? And when are you going to pay for the room?" Fayuan said nothing.

Here is one of the most important passages in this section. In our day-to-day life, where it is possible to defend or explain our actions, then I think we ought to do so. But there are times when defending ourselves or attempting to explain our situation just doesn't work. At those times, what else is there to do but shut up and die?

Once there was a monk in our sangha named Dōki Zentetsu, who was conscripted during the war. Just before he died in battle, we received a long letter from him. He wrote, "There are many young men like myself here who could get shot at any moment. I really wonder about the sanity of it all, but if I do get hit, what else can I do but shut up and die?"

It's important to try to keep alive by staying out of the line of fire, but there come times when you find yourself standing right in it. Life just isn't so cut-and-dried that it's possible for us to eliminate that possibility. So far I've been fortunate enough to have lived for many years, and for that I have to be grateful. Yet I always knew the day could arrive when there would be nothing else for me to do but be still and die. And there are times when defending yourself just doesn't work and there is nothing else to do but be quiet and take whatever comes.

A person who feels he has to defend himself every time his teacher says something to him isn't really practicing Buddhism. There are times when an evaluation or criticism by others hits home, but then there are other times when it's way off the mark. If it's correct, then you ought to sit on it for a while and consider the matter. If it isn't, then it should be enough for you to tell yourself it's off the mark and let it go at that. If you aren't able to forget criticism by others, how can you really be living out the full reality of your life? To practice Buddhism means to confront and live out the reality of your life, so if some unwarranted criticism comes along, your practice is to live it out by not getting all in a lather over it.

Fayuan went around the town as a mendicant, carrying his bowl for donations, and returned in full all the money he owed the temple. One day Guixing happened to see Fayuan out on his rounds with his bowl. Returning to the monastery, the abbot told the monks that Fayuan truly possessed the attitude of one who is seeking the Way. Shortly after, he sent a message to Fayuan allowing him to return to the temple.

Finally Guixing let him back in and even praised him, but confidentially, Guixing seems a bit too severe for me.

To be sure, what Fayuan did was technically wrong. Yet when the whole community was suffering from malnutrition, it was vital to have the kind of spirit he had. Of course, be careful that you don't go out and twist what I've said to mean that stealing from others is perfectly all right. You have to remember that after Fayuan stole the noodles from the storage room and Guixing told him to pay for it, Fayuan didn't just fold up. He went out and paid dearly for it.

If someone comes along who's completely at a loss as to what to do and asks for advice, as a bodhisattva you can't just say that you don't know, it's not your problem. That's shirking your responsibility. Not taking responsibility for what you say or do is the safest way out. But when someone's all mixed up, what choice have you but to reply with the best advice you can?

You should know that it's not enough for a bodhisattva to just uphold the precepts. There are times when you have to break them, too. It's just that when you do, you have to do so with the resolve of also being willing to accept whatever consequences may follow. That's what "together with all sentient beings," *issai shujō to tomo ni,* means—together regardless of what hell one might fall into.

With the whole monastery suffering from malnutrition, who wouldn't do what Fayuan did? Up to the point where he took the key and stole the food from the storage room, he looks like Robin Hood, and it is not such an unusual story. But Guixing is in a completely different position. He had to find out if Fayuan took the noodles merely to enhance his own reputation in the monastery or if he did it fully willing to accept the consequences. That's why Guixing had to be so severe.

So Guixing carried out his role as the leader of the community, and Fayuan bore the burden for what he had done. It's not enough just to know the definition of bodhisattva. You have to study the actions of a bodhisattva and then behave like one.

Regarding the question "What is a bodhisattva?" you could also define a bodhisattva as one who acts as a true adult. That is, most people in the world act like children. There is a chapter in the *Shōbōgenzō* entitled "Eight Aspects of an Enlightened Being" *(Hachi Dainin Gaku).* The word *dainin* means "true adult" or "bodhisattva." Today most people who are called adults are only pseudo-adults. Physically, they grow up and become adult, but spiritually too many people never mature to adulthood. They don't behave as adults in their daily lives. A bodhisattva is one who sees the world through adult eyes and whose actions are the actions of a true adult.

Magnanimous Mind

What it means concretely to live and work as a bodhisattva, waking up to universal self—this is the question Dōgen Zenji addresses in the *Regulations for Eihei Monastery*. This book was considered so indispensable by the followers of Dōgen that they carried it with them wherever they went. When living in a monastery they constantly reread it as a guide to their activities. I believe that it is a truly incomparable religious text that gives practical guidance regarding how to put zazen into practice in our daily lives. In the first chapter, called "Instructions for the Cook" *(Tenzo Kyōkun)*, Dōgen Zenji speaks of the spirit of the bodhisattva's actual life in terms of three minds or attitudes toward life: magnanimous mind, nurturing mind, and joyful mind.[60]

To look at what is meant by magnanimous mind—or, in Japanese, *daishin*—we need to look at how we see others when we experience the reality of life itself. This reality of life is self connected to all things. Through it we live that life of the whole self that has no limit and that nothing is outside of, so no matter what happens, we are always living out the life of self that is only self.

One might reason that it may well be possible to be one true self that is only true self during zazen, when we can put down our work and discontinue communicating and associating with other people, but that it is impossible to be that self in our daily lives with other people and the outside world existing right in front of us.

But it isn't a matter of becoming just universal self by means of some special device whereby we erase all the other people who are before us. Rather, the reality of life is that we are always living out the true self that is only the true self, just as during zazen.

We assume that we are all living together in one commonly shared world. However, this is not true from the perspective of the reality of our actual life-experience, which we learn about through letting go of our thoughts in zazen. For example, when you and I look at a cup, we usually assume that we are looking at the very same cup, but this isn't so in terms of true, raw life-experience. I am looking from my angle and with my power of vision and you are looking from your angle and with your power of vision. There is absolutely no way we can exchange nor understand each other's experience.

This is not only true for seeing; it is true of every perception and sense experience—hearing, smelling, tasting, and touching. The world in which we actually live and experience life in its vivid freshness is a world that is mine alone and yours alone. This holds true even more for our thoughts. As in the proverb "Several men, several minds," everyone has completely different thoughts, just as everyone has a completely different face. Even though people who believe in the same doctrine use the same slogans and follow the same formalized way of thinking, there can be no doubt that behind those expressions their understanding in terms of vivid reality is as varied as they are. If we assume that all of humanity is living in the same world and has the same ideas, this is a crucial mistake. Even when it seems that we are communicating because we are using the same words, this is communication only in a generalized and abstract sense. In terms of raw life-experience everyone lives in a different world and lives out his or her own world of self that is only self.

We often say things like "I know you very well." But this hardly means that I know everything about you. It only means that I know the aspect of you that appears before me. For me, you are nothing but the *you* that is within my world, within the universal self as my world.

When we talk about vivid life-experience in which we let go of our thoughts, this is not limited only to the times when we are doing zazen, it applies equally to our daily lives. Living out universal self at all times is not some special thing, it is a most natural and fundamental reality for all of us. Having become habituated to give and take with "others" whom we have arbitrarily fabricated in our own minds, we have lost sight of the truth in terms of vivid life-experience. The most concrete and readily understandable example of this is the way people in society think about money. Money has no value beyond the one created by the promises people make in their heads, yet most people think of money as reality, losing sight of the reality of the universal self that is their own self.

If we take a fresh look through our zazen and practice living out the reality of fresh and immediate life, then it will be clear to anyone that whatever happens, there is nothing outside of living out self that is only self. This is what is called magnanimous mind, the attitude that never discriminates. Without discriminating in terms of "I like that, I don't like this, I want that, I don't want this," since everything I encounter lies within my life-experience, I look on everything equally as my life. My life is not limited to the physical pulsation of my heart. My life is in every experience—that is, everywhere life functions. Every way I encounter life manifesting as life, that is my life-experience. That is why in Buddhism "self settling on itself" is the same as the universe settling on itself! The magnanimous mind of a bodhisattva sees the self as one with the universe, and since everything we encounter is our life, we seek to manifest that life regardless of what it is or what happens, without discrimination.

With this magnanimous mind, which throws out the thoughts of the small self and ceases to discriminate, it becomes clear that my whole world appears before me as my present circumstances, the scenery of my life, the content of my own self that is also the whole self. This is exactly the same as in zazen, where all the thoughts that come and go are the scenery of zazen.

The very same thing can be said about time. Usually we assume that time is something that is flowing from the past, through the present, and toward the future, and that we live within time. However, if we think about this in terms of raw life-experience, we realize that this is not at all so. The past has already gone by and doesn't exist, and the future hasn't come yet, so it doesn't exist, either. Actually, there is just this one moment of the present; our ideas of past and future are nothing but the scenery that floats into our minds within this momentary present. One might be tempted to say that this isn't true, since "old" things like buildings and books are right here and now. However, as the reality of life, these buildings and books exist only in the present, and thinking that they are "old" is nothing but the present thought in my head. In other words, my currently existing head gives the attribute of "old" to the buildings and books that exist right now. In terms of raw life-experience we are always living out the present that is only the present, the now that is only now.

So what in the world does it mean to live and work as universal self? Clearly, it is living and working in the now that is only now, as the self that is only self, no matter what happens. Whatever we are now faced with is what lives and functions as our life. With this attitude toward life there is no past, future, or other person before the eyes of our self, there is only living out the reality of ever-present life.

The Direction of the Universal

The reality of life that zazen wakes us up to is actually a life attitude of working and living out a self that is only self, a now that is only now. It is an attitude of facing whatever is before us, regardless of what might befall us.

What a vast, boundless life unfolds before us! Ordinarily, we spend all our time comparing and discriminating between this and that, always looking around for something good to happen to us. Because of that, we become restless and anxious about everything. As long as we are able to imagine something better than what we have or who we are, it follows naturally that there could also be something worse. We are constantly pursued by anxious misgivings that something bad will happen. As long as we base our lives on distinguishing between the better way and the worse way, we can never find absolute peace such that whatever happens is all right.

When we let go of our thoughts that distinguish better from worse and instead see everything in terms of the universal self, we are able to settle upon a different attitude toward life—the attitude of magnanimous mind that whatever happens, we are living out self alone. Here a truly peaceful life unfolds.

In Pure Land and some older schools of Buddhism, we hear about paradise and hell, and in Christianity, heaven and hell. In our day-to-day lives, we hear about happiness and unhappiness, or fortunate circumstances and unfortunate ones. We assume it to be perfectly natural that heaven, happiness, and fortunate circumstances are good, and that hell, unhappiness, and unfortunate circumstances are *bad*. This type of categorization or discrimination is nothing but a distinction we make in our minds and is totally removed from the reality of life. Yet precisely because of these distinctions, we get all excited over wanting to go a better way and trying not to go some worse way. As long as we act like this, we completely lose sight of absolute peace.

The important point here in terms of the truth of universal self is not to run away from the worse way (hell, unhappiness, or bad circumstances) and turn toward some better way (heaven, happiness, or good circumstances) by discriminating between better and worse using our heads. Rather, what is crucial is magnanimous mind, with which we take the attitude of living straight through whatever reality of life we are presently faced with. In other words, if I fall into hell, then hell itself is my life at that time, so I have to live right through it, and if I find myself in heaven, then heaven is my life and I have to live right through that.

When we settle on an attitude toward life whereby universal self lives out its own reality of life, I do not mean to imply that heaven and hell, or happiness and unhappiness, cease to exist, but that it becomes clear that all these are just the scenery of our lives. In the life of the whole self, various scenery unfolds, but the absolute reality, the undeniable fact, is that whatever happens, self lives out self that is only self.

Whatever happens in our lives can be accepted, since we are universal self in all circumstances. You may imagine that this will leave you completely directionless, but this is not the case, since such a self is not devoid of scenery. Self as the reality of life unfolds the rich quality of life: the scenery of the self, the circumstances of the present. Both past and future exist as the richly textured scenery of the present.

Usually, we do not understand these circumstances of the present moment as the scenery that unfolds within the universal self. Instead, we analyze this *now*. We place ourselves within the illusive flow of time from past to future and become bound by our relationships with others, bound by the force of habit of the past, and bound by our goals for the future. Being totally tied up, we are dragged around by the expectations of our small egos and end up floundering in desperation.

When we see everything as the scenery and circumstances of the here and now, how do we function as universal self within this moment? Through the life circumstances of this self that is at once our personal self and the whole self of the universe, we act in a lively and vivid way by giving life to the past in terms of our own wealth of experiences and by responding to directions toward the future.

As long as we wake up and live as universal self, we work in the direction where all things are alive. And since everything we encounter is our life, with the attitude or spirit that our whole self is taking care of its own life we aim at giving life to all things, all situations, all people, all worlds. This is nurturing mind— *rōshin* in Japanese—the mind of a parent looking after its child, described in the "Instructions to the Head Cook." I live by giving life to you, and within this the universal lives, because you and I and all things are already living nothing else but that life which is connected to everything—universal life. This nurturing mind is the natural functioning of magnanimous mind, with which we work to enable the flower of life to bloom in every encounter.

In winter in Japan, all the plants die back, but suddenly when spring comes, many varieties of wildflowers bloom in the fields. Each of these wildflowers is blooming forth the life of spring. From the other side, by the coming of the life we call spring, the violet blooms as a violet, the dandelion as a dandelion, the lotus as a lotus.

In the same way, the flower of my life blossoms when I work to make the flower that is the world, people, and things I now face blossom. And within the blossoming of the flowers of my life, the flowers of all things come to blossom. Likewise, the flower of your life blossoms when you work to enable the flowers you now face to blossom, and therein blooms the flower of universal life.

The flow of universal life is stifled by an attitude that sets up this world as just a place to compete for survival, one in which people merely rise and fall. This attitude sees the law of survival of the fittest as absolute truth and within that framework manifests a spirit of comparing, rating, and competing with others, kicking one another down the ladder, winning and losing. It sees winners degenerating in their own extravagance and losers going from frustration to neurosis. People with such an attitude end up unable to make their own flower blossom. How can universal life bloom in this environment?

I have been speaking of *the blooming of the flower of life*, but this is not a matter of setting up a goal of making a flower bloom and then achieving that goal. The manifestation of this universal life force is the direction life takes, but it is never activity directed toward goals, since goals are necessarily outside or beyond us as we are now. A delineated goal does not exist for universal life. There is only the direction of the force of life.

This is equally true in zazen as the practice of the Buddha Way. If in our practice we try to achieve some goal by means of zazen, even if the goal is satori, then we have become completely separated from true zazen and practice. Precisely because we live the life of universal self, we just practice and manifest that life force. In this sense, our attitude of arousing the mind of the bodhisattva and of practicing should not be one of moving toward some goal; rather, it should be an attitude of purely manifesting life.

The reality of life changes moment by moment. Therefore, self must work in the encounter of every moment and in the direction of the manifestation of the life that pervades all things. Here is where we come to find the true value of life—living out the whole self no matter what happens. In the "Instructions to the Head Cook" this is referred to as joyful mind, or *kishin,* the mind that lives in accord with the true value of life. Joyful mind comes up as a dynamic feeling of truly being alive. Joyful mind does not mean a feeling of excitement at the fulfillment of some desire. Rather, joyful mind is discovering one's worth and passion for life through the action of parental mind toward everything we encounter. When we see each encounter as our life, and function with the spirit that each and every encounter is our child to be looked after and taken care of, we will discover true ardor and passion and joy in being alive. Right there we will become true adults. Any bodhisattva aspiring to live the Way of Buddha will without exception possess these three minds of magnanimity, joy, and parental care.

Dōgen Zenji's "Only Buddha Together with Buddha" (Shōbō-genzō Yuibutsu-yobutsu) casts a clear light on this:

> All the buddhas have completed their practice, become one with the Way, and attained enlightenment. How are we to understand the identity of ourselves and the buddhas? The practice of the buddhas is carried on together with the whole world and all sentient beings. If it is not universal, it is not the practice of the buddhas. Therefore, from the time we first aspire to the Way until we attain buddhahood, both practice and attainment of buddhahood must be one with the whole world and all sentient beings.

A present-day person aspiring to find a true way of life will meet all the problems of modern society. Human progress is by no means the same as the advancement of natural science; nor does it follow the path of the development of material civilization. Human progress lies in each and every human being becoming an adult.

Becoming an adult is nothing other than each one of us becoming a bodhisattva, where we see every encounter as our child and discover our joy and ardor in life through looking after each of our children. When this becomes a world of bodhisattva adults in which we watch over one another and care for and help each other, then humanity will have come of age and we may rightly say we have progressed. I propose that a bodhisattva, protected and guided by zazen and living by vow and repentance, must be the true ideal image of a human being for the coming age.

Living

Wide

Awake

—

137

The Wayseeker

In February 1975 Uchiyama Roshi gave his last lecture at Antaiji before retiring as abbot. It was snowing heavily that day, and a hundred people listened for over two hours to his farewell address, "The Wayseeker," in which he tried to pass on to all his followers a clear direction for practicing true dharma.

Seven Points of Practice

1. Study and practice the buddhadharma only for the sake of the buddhadharma, not for the sake of emotions or worldly ideas.

2. Zazen is our truest and most venerable teacher.

3. Zazen must work concretely in our daily lives as the two practices (vow and repentance), the three minds (magnanimous mind, nurturing mind, and joyful mind), and as the realization of the saying "Gaining is delusion, losing is enlightenment."

4. Live by vow and root it deeply.

5. Realizing that development and backsliding are your responsibility alone, endeavor to practice and develop.

6. Sit silently for ten years, then for ten more years, and then for another ten years.

7. Cooperate with one another and aim to create a place where sincere practitioners can practice without trouble.

1. Study and practice the buddhadharma only for the sake of the buddhadharma, not for the sake of emotions or worldly ideas

This is the most important point for us as students of Zen. No one emphasized practicing buddhadharma only for the sake of the buddhadharma more than Dōgen Zenji. I think the most important expression in his teaching is *buddhadharma*. Despite that, we've become so familiar with the expression that we often pass over it without considering what it really means.

At the very start of Dōgen's *Genjō Kōan* ("The Koan of Being in the Present," from the *Shōbōgenzō*) are the words "When all dharmas are the buddhadharma." The essence of Dōgen Zenji's teaching is buddhadharma. We should start, therefore, by examining just what it really is.

The famous koan of the Chinese master Shitou Xiqian (in Japanese, Sekitō Kisen) "no gaining, no knowing" is one of the best expressions of the meaning of buddhadharma. This koan is in the *Shōbōgenzō: Sanbyaku-soku* or *Shinji Shōbōgenzō (Collection of Three Hundred Koans)* compiled by Dōgen Zenji. Shitou was one of the great Zen masters of the flowering of Zen in China in the eighth century. He was asked by one of his disciples, Tianhuang Daowu:

"What is the essential meaning of buddhadharma?"

Shitou replied, "No gaining, no knowing."

Daowu asked again, "Can you say anything further?"

Shitou answered, "The expansive sky does not obstruct the floating white clouds."

The wide expanse of the sky does not obstruct the passing clouds. It lets them float freely. I think these words from the koan fully express the meaning of buddhadharma.

At first Shitou answered "No gaining, no knowing" to the question "What is the essential meaning of buddhadharma?" From looking at the Chinese it might appear that he said "I don't know." But that's not what he meant. He meant "No gaining, no knowing *is* buddhadharma." "No gaining, no knowing" is the attitude of refraining from all fabrication. In other words, it means to be free from the ideas we make up in our head. I call this opening the hand of thought.

When we think of something, we grasp it with our minds. If we open the hand of thought, it drops away. This is Dōgen Zenji's famous phrase *shinjin datsuraku* ("dropping off body and mind"). Hearing the words *dropping off body and mind,* many people imagine something like their body becoming unhinged and falling apart. This is not what it means. When we open the hand of thought, the things made up inside our heads fall away; that's the meaning of dropping off body and mind.

The expression "opening the hand of thought" is on a par with the ancient masters' finest phrases. For example, Zen Master Bankei coined the expression *unborn buddha mind (fusshō no busshin)*. This line was wonderful three hundred years ago, but "unborn buddha mind" doesn't mean much to people these days.

Bankei said that all problems are resolved with unborn buddha mind. In the same way, all problems are resolved by opening the hand of thought. When we try to put everything in order using only our brains, we never succeed. Since all our troubles are caused by our discriminating minds, we should open the hand of thought. This is body and mind dropping off. That is when all our troubles disappear. There is a short poem that says:

> When the quarrel over water
> Reaches its highest pitch
> —a sudden rain.

People are fighting with each other, each family trying to draw more water into its own paddy field during a dry summer. At the height of the conflict, it suddenly gets cloudy, starts thundering, and big drops of rain begin to fall. The rain resolves the fundamental cause of the fight.

In the same way, if we think something is a big problem—for example, which of two things we should choose—we struggle to resolve it in our heads. But if we open the hand of thought, the problem itself dissolves. When we are sitting, we open the hand of thought and let all our thoughts come and go freely.

"What is the essential meaning of buddhadharma?"

"No gaining, no knowing."

This koan describes what zazen is quite well. What on earth is buddhadharma? Fundamentally, it is just opening the hand of thought. And to practice opening the hand of thought concretely with the body and mind is zazen.

We can also say that buddhadharma is the dharma (reality or truth) realized by a buddha. The word "buddha" means "one who has awakened." So buddhadharma means "what awareness is," or perhaps "way of awareness."

What is this way of awareness? Let us first consider what it means to be unaware, or oblivious to what is going on around us. All human beings are deluded by our brains and become absentminded because of our discriminating minds. One of the many varieties of absentmindedness is falling asleep. This is not so serious, because to awaken from sleep we need do nothing more than be full of vigor. We also get caught up in desire, anger, and group stupidity.[61] These are more difficult to deal with, because they are fabrications conjured up in our heads. We create various illusions in our minds and then jump in, becoming immersed in them. There used to be a dense growth of bamboo at a place in Japan called Yawata, in Chiba Prefecture. Once you lost your way in it, you could never find your way out, so there's an expression, *Yawata no yabushirazu*—"Being totally lost in the bamboo thicket of Yawata." We human beings make up illusions and then become lost and confused in the jungle we ourselves have created.

How can we awaken from these illusions? The only way is to open the hand of thought, because our thoughts themselves are the source of illusion. When we let go of our thoughts and become vividly aware, all the illusions that create desire, anger, and group stupidity vanish immediately. This is the way of awareness. We must neither fall asleep nor get carried away by our thoughts. The essential point in zazen is to *be* vividly aware, opening the hand of thought.

Buddhism emphasizes two principles of life: impermanence (*mujō*), and that all phenomena are the results of causation and are without permanent or independent substance *(engishojō)*. In other words, the reality of life changes from moment to moment, and there is no unchanging substance. Since antiquity people have said that a diamond cannot be destroyed and have used it as a symbol of "absolute permanence," but in fact a diamond is simply compressed carbon, which is combustible. Furthermore, modern science has shown that elementary particles are always changing. Everything is constantly changing. The reality of the impermanence that we awaken to is satori, yet some people aim at shooting down and carting home a ready-made satori or enlightenment, like some kind of trophy. It's impossible.

The only true enlightenment is awareness of the vivid reality of life, moment by moment. So we practice enlightenment right now, right here, in every moment. This attitude is expressed in the phrase "practice and enlightenment are one" *(shushō ichinyo)*. It is an essential point of Dōgen Zenji's teaching not to obtain enlightenment as a result of practice, but to be vividly aware and to open the hand of thought from moment to moment, because it is our thought that binds us. You should understand this true enlightenment of buddhadharma. Enlightenment is not like a sudden realization of something mysterious. Enlightenment is nothing but awakening from illusions and returning to the reality of life.

What Dōgen Zenji meant by the phrase "practice and enlightenment are one," Shakyamuni Buddha called precepts, or *pratimoksha* (Sanskrit). In The Sutra of the Last Discourse, which was Shakyamuni Buddha's final teaching just before his death, there is a passage that reads:

Monks, after my death, respect and follow the *pratimoksha*.

If you do, you will be like a person who has been given a light in the dark, or like a pauper who acquires a great treasure.

These are Shakyamuni Buddha's last words. He said his disciples should respect and follow the precepts. *Pratimoksa* has been translated into Japanese not just simply as "precepts" but also as "emancipation through the observance of the precepts" *(shosho gedatsu* or *betsubetsu gedatsu).*[62] Each precept that is kept liberates us from its corresponding evil. Where we observe a particular precept, there we are immediately emancipated.

I think this idea of *pratimoksha* is the origin of Dōgen Zenji's "practice and enlightenment are one." *Betsubetsu gedatsu* means that if we uphold a certain precept, we will be emancipated to the extent of that precept. If we open the hand of thought right here, right now, and experience reality, that is true enlightenment. Dōgen expressed the spirit of Shakyamuni Buddha in his own words when he said "practice and enlightenment are one."

It seems that very few people who study Buddhism these days pay any attention to the idea of *pratimoksha*—I asked some students from a Buddhist university whether they knew about *pratimoksha* or not, but none of them had heard of it. Shakyamuni Buddha said very clearly that after his death his disciples should respect *pratimoksha* more than anything else, so it must be very important. This spirit of *pratimoksha* is the same as that expressed in "practice and enlightenment are one." Therefore, instead of aiming at some ready-made enlightenment, we should practice opening the hand of thought and just be aware of the vivid reality of life in every place and in every moment. This is buddhadharma.

What does "practicing buddhadharma only for the sake of bud-dharma" mean? As I said before, it means to practice opening the hand of thought. For example, we usually grasp the idea of life and death with our thinking minds. As people get older, they often express their fear of death. When they were young, they never thought about the fact that sooner or later they were going to die. But now, as they grow old and death is approaching, they suddenly remember. They get scared and agonize over what to do. They are seized with fear because they are only thinking about death; life and death are both just ideas in their heads. They assume that when a living being dies, it must be painful. Pondering life and death within the illusions they've fabricated throughout their lives, they become paralyzed with fear. In reality, life and death don't take place in our heads. They occur beyond human thought. They occur where the hand of thought is open.

To practice opening the hand of thought, right now, right here, knowing that the reality of life is beyond human thought—that is what it means to practice buddhadharma only for the sake of the buddhadharma. It is definitely not to practice letting go of thought for the purpose of gaining some utilitarian reward conjured up in your head. If you practice zazen to become healthy, tough, or brave, you are going in an entirely wrong direction.

A Westerner visiting Japan came to see me and asked if we could attain spontaneity through practicing zazen. I thought it was a strange question. Someone told me that spontaneity was really popular among Americans who practiced zazen. I suppose someone translated the Buddhist term *zenki* as "spontaneity." So I understood the question to mean: Can zazen help us gain, for example, the power to shout "Katsu!" the way Rinzai did? I replied that I didn't need such point-less spontaneity and that if you are really spontaneous, you don't need to chase after such nonsense. If a bill collector comes around demanding his money, it's very convenient if you can shout "Katsu!" to chase him away. It's very handy in terms of your human feelings. You'll feel gratified in your deluded mind. But this kind of human emotion has nothing to do with buddhadharma. You have to understand that practicing the buddhadharma is nothing like drinking a bottle of soda pop and feeling refreshed. People want the buddhadharma to be useful or to satisfy their desires. That's no good. The true Buddha Way is to practice buddhadharma for its own sake.

If you think the most important thing in your system of values is something made up in your head, you're totally wrong. What is most valuable isn't fabricated in our heads: it arises when we open the hand of thought. Opening the hand of thought *is itself* what is most valuable. This is the meaning of "practicing buddhadharma only for the sake of the buddhadharma."

There are too many teachers who don't make any effort to transmit the buddhadharma only for the sake of the buddhadharma. They attract people by dangling some attractive carrot in front of them and then claim that by practicing zazen you can acquire great powers, but that is not true zazen, no matter how hard you practice it. True zazen is not practiced for the sake of some value promoted by desire. Anything our discriminating minds believe to be valuable is not of absolute value. Letting go, opening the hand of thought, is the reality of life; and it is that reality of life which should be most valuable to us.

In Paul's Letter to the Romans he says, "Let God be true though every man be false" (3:4). A lot of people get very uncomfortable when I quote anything from the Bible, but important sayings are important, and this one is certainly true. In reference to our practice, everything we make up in our heads is false; "opening the hand of thought" should be our standard of absolute value. We should respect the buddhadharma of letting go of thought as being most valuable. So it is important not to practice for the sake of sentimental emotions or worldly ideas.

At the same time, we should be careful of a potential trap in this attitude. When people hear that they shouldn't practice for the sake of human emotions or worldly ideas, sometimes they try to separate buddhadharma from these things completely and they fence off a small area of existence as buddhadharma. For example, as part of one of the esoteric practices of the Shingon school, a special place is marked off and various items are displayed on a special altar for making burnt offerings. They think of these as the only holy places of the buddhadharma. There are others who set aside some mountains as holy and prohibit women, because women are somehow considered impure, but this is just human discrimination. This kind of attitude is completely different from that expressed in "the expansive sky does not obstruct the floating white clouds."

In more complicated cases, people insist on buddhadharma as being something special in order to boost their own egos. There are a lot of teachers who talk of buddhadharma only for the sake of buddhadharma as a kind of smoke screen behind which they are secretly just trying to get their own way. This point requires a great deal of caution. The basis of buddhadharma is "The expansive sky does not obstruct the floating white clouds." We must neither oppose nor deny the existence of human emotions and worldly ideas.

What this boils down to is the importance of following the buddhadharma only for the sake of buddhadharma. We practitioners must maintain an attitude of practicing buddhadharma only for the sake of buddhadharma, without justifying it by human emotions and worldly ideas. No one can stop people from saying you did such-and-such contrary to buddhadharma for the sake of buddhadharma, but it is not a standard for judging people. Quite a few priests go astray on this point, spouting fancy words for the sake of their own cravings. For example, they'll talk about generosity, or the perfection of giving (Skt., *dana-paramita)*, as being the chief virtue, and tell you how you should practice it. Then they pocket your money for themselves! This is inexcusable. We can't demand that others practice generosity without practicing it ourselves.

The most important point in Buddhism is that each of us practices it ourselves. We must apply every teaching and every practice to ourselves. In understanding buddhadharma for the sake of buddhadharma, this attitude is essential.

2. Zazen is our truest and most venerable teacher

The enshrined buddha statue on an altar is referred to as the *honzon*, but the word really means "what is most revered." What is of highest value and most worthy of veneration is the zazen of opening the hand of thought.

Once a visitor to Antaiji wanted to pay reverence to the buddha statue in the zendo. When I opened the door, he was surprised to see an electric fan above the altar and exclaimed that it was irreverent to put a fan above the Buddha. People in Kyoto think that the buddha statue is the most venerable thing in a temple. But in Antaiji, the *honzon* is on the other side of the hall, in the activity of zazen. The electric fan is installed above the buddha statue to keep the room cool in the summer for the people who sit. It's important to keep the room cool in the summer and warm in the winter. The buddha statue is just an embodiment of zazen as the most venerable thing. Opening the hand of thought for oneself should have ultimate value.

If we're not careful, we are apt to grant ultimate value to something we've just made up in our heads. Worldly types are always in a haze, thinking that money, fame, or status is the most valuable thing. Since we sometimes become absentminded and forget what is most important, we need to practice and reflect upon ourselves continually. This is what I mean by saying zazen is the most venerable thing in our lives.

This applies equally well to the notion of a true or genuine teacher—in Japanese, *shōshi*. Dōgen Zenji said, "If you cannot find a true teacher, it is better not to practice."[63] Who or what is a true teacher, then? If we mull it over in our heads and decide that so-and-so must be a true teacher, we're making a big mistake. We're only trusting our misguided thought that a certain person is a true teacher.

Zazen, which is letting go and opening the hand of thought, is the only true teacher. This is an important point. I have never said to my disciples that I am a true teacher. From the beginning I have said that the zazen each of us practices is the only true teacher.

Since Sawaki Roshi passed away, I have been giving dharma lectures *(teishō)* to my disciples. But this is just my role. I've never said that I am a true teacher or that I am always right. Whether you think I am a true teacher or not is only your opinion. A true teacher is just not that sort of thing. Please do not forget that the zazen of opening the hand of thought is what constitutes our true teacher and is most worthy of respect.

3. Zazen must work concretely in our daily lives as the two practices (vow and repentance), the three minds (magnani-

mous mind, nurturing mind, and joyful mind), and as the realization of the saying "Gaining is delusion, losing is enlightenment."

Some people believe that all activities that use the same posture as zazen are alike, but there are many different kinds of sitting practices. Southeast Asian Buddhists practice sitting meditation. Non-Buddhist practices like yoga have sitting practices. Altogether, there are quite a number of such practices. The posture may be the same, but the spirit and purpose are different.

What I am attempting to do through all my writings is to clarify just what true zazen is. And, of course, it is even more important to train people who can teach true zazen directly. These two things—writing and teaching my students—have been my most important work for many years. Fortunately, the number of disciples who can teach is growing, for which I am grateful.

As I have said, the content of our zazen is determined by our attitude toward it. Our zazen is not the practice of so-called "zen of the six realms" *(rokudō zen)*. That is "lowercase *Z*" zen, not true Zen. Six-realms zen is made up of hell-realm zen *(jigoku zen)*, insatiable-spirit zen *(gaki zen)*, animal zen *(chikushō zen)*, fighting-spirit zen *(shura zen)*, humanistic zen *(ningen zen)*, and heavenly-being zen *(tenjō zen)*.

What is hell-realm zen? Well, there are some people who are afraid of even the sound of the word "zazen," and a surprising number of these people are Zen priests! Some monks stay at officially recognized training monasteries *(senmon sōdō)* for a certain period to receive a certificate that enables them to run a temple of their own. Although they hate zazen, they are forced to sit while they are training. This is as miserable for them as being in hell. After they get their certificate they never do zazen again if they can help it. Doing zazen with that kind of attitude is really meaningless.

Insatiable spirits are those whose hungers can never be satisfied no matter how much they consume. This is the zazen of people who chase after enlightenment with the desperation of starving ghosts.

The third type of zen is animal zen, in the sense of dumb brutes or domesticated animals like dogs and cats. Let's face it, there are some people who stay in monasteries because as long as they follow along, they are fed. Occasionally, this type strays into Antaiji. They stay here because they can get fed; they sit sesshins just to kill time. Domestic-animal zen is a waste of time, and this kind of person should be tossed out. It is particularly pointless to try to be a house pet at Antaiji, where we do not serve fancy tidbits. There is a Japanese expression *yoraba taiju no kage,* which means to look for shelter under the shade of a big tree. It's a terrible mistake to take shelter at Antaiji; it's like trying to relax in the shade under a patch of grass.

Fourth, we have the zen of combative demons. This is the zen in which people compete over who is most enlightened or whose practice is most severe. They beat each other with the *kyōsaku* (meditation stick) to show how tough they are.

Then comes humanistic zen. This is zazen practiced for utilitarian reasons. Some people sit to get their heads straight, to improve their health, and so on. There are an awful lot of books published like *Zen for Health* or *Zen as Psychotherapy.* This is zen out to improve humanity on the basis of human values. People who always expect to get something in return, a quid pro quo for their effort, are practicing this kind of zen.

The sixth type is heavenly zen. The people who practice this want to be hermits or saints. Lots of Americans seem drawn to this type of zen. I guess they want to escape from the noisy, materialistic society of America and live in remote mountains enjoying the silence. This is zen undertaken as a hobby or a fad. It has absolutely nothing to do with the buddhadharma.

To recognize true zazen, we have to look at our practice from an absolute perspective. If you are caught up in one of the limited kinds of zen of the six realms, you can no longer see the essential point of buddhadharma. And what is that? As I said before, Buddhism teaches impermanence and the quality of non-ego. Letting go and opening the hand of thought is the foundation of Zen based on the buddhadharma.

The saying "gaining is delusion, losing is enlightenment" has very practical value. In our ordinary human life, we are always trying to fulfill our desires. We're satisfied only when all our desires are met. In Buddhism, though, it's just the opposite: it is important for us to leave our desires alone, without trying to fulfill them. If we push this one step further—*gaining is delusion, losing is enlightenment*—we're talking about active participation in loss.

Let me be clear that I am not saying, "Losing is important, so go help people out by collecting what you can from them." That just makes you the "someone" who gains. Rather, apply this saying just to yourself and give something up. For breaking the ego's grip, nothing is more effective than giving something up.

We need to remind ourselves of the clear distinction between personal, conditioned self and universal, original self.[64] The personal self is what we usually think of as "I." But if we peel away the skin of this individual, conditioned self, we lay bare the original, universal self. The personal self is always trying to fulfill its desires; this is the so-called karmic self. Human beings are born with brains, and we naturally have a tendency (or karma) that leads us to fabricate a maze of illusions in our minds. This is our individual self, but it's a big mistake to assume that this self is the whole self. The whole self appears when we strip away karmic illusions. And that means "opening the hand of thought." This is original, universal self.

There is a koan that asks, "What is your original face before your parents were born?" One might naturally assume that there is some special thing called "original face," but that is not the right approach. When we open the hand of thought, letting go, the original self is already there. It's not some special mystical state. Don't seek it somewhere else. When we open the hand of thought, what is there, in that moment, is our original face. When we refrain from grasping our thoughts, we realize that the force that animates our lives and the force that moves the wind are the very same force. Our lives and the force that moves the wind are the same. Our breath and the wind blowing are one.

Ordinarily, we think we are alive because our brains are in control. This is a grave mistake. The range our brains control is pretty limited. We drink a cup of tea when our brains conceive of wanting to drink something. We can do this as our brain orders us to. But generally, only things such as our hands, legs, and tongue consistently follow the orders issued by our brains. It's virtually impossible to exercise total control over our hearts or our lungs. We breathe in our sleep. It's not really a personal effort. When we're asleep, we open the hand of thought, breathing without worrying about it. I breathe even when my brain isn't conscious of it, don't I? This certainly is me. All this, all our life activity of mind and body, is the original self.

A word that Dōgen Zenji uses throughout the *Shōbōgenzō* to strengthen other words is *jin,* which means whole, exhaustive, or all-inclusive. Dōgen frequently uses expressions like *jin jippō kai* ("the whole-ten-direction-world"), *jinissai* ("everything"), and *jinchi, jinkai, jinji, jippō* ("the whole earth, all worlds, all time, the whole dharma"). In short, it means something that includes everything. In other words, my life. Our real life is connected to everything. Our minds conceive of "I" as only "myself," as something independent. But if we open the hand of thought, such a conception vanishes and we can realize "I" as being one with everything.

It's incredibly difficult to understand this life that is one with all things. I have been practicing zazen for some thirty years since becoming a monk, and the one thing that is gradually becoming clearer to me is that "I" am one with everything, completely beyond considerations of usefulness. Sawaki Roshi used to say, "Zazen really is useless in terms of being utilitarian or beneficial to you or society." Zazen is good for nothing; it really is useless. But the longer I practice, the clearer it becomes to me that nothing is separated from me. Please try it and see: if you put your whole energy into practicing zazen, continually opening the hand of thought, you will clearly see that you are connected to everything.

Where do we go after death? Nowhere. Life is universal. When we're born, we come from this universal life. We are all, without exception, universal. Only our brains get caught up in the notion that we are individual. We're universal whether we think so or not, and reality doesn't care what we think.

As long as we are living, we eat cabbage and rice, bread and wine. Our bodies are collections of such stuff. Superficially, it seems that our bodies are separate from the rest of the world. But as a matter of fact, our bodies continuously radiate heat and moisture and absorb nutrients and light. Everything is coming and going with remarkable freedom. We really are universal. Where are we going after death? Back to universal life. That's why the Japanese refer to the recently deceased as *shin ki gen* ("one who has returned to the origin"). This universal life is the original self.

It's no use saying that everything except what our brains come up with is universal. Thinking is also one of the functions of the universal self. However, our brains can think of things that don't exist. For example, I can think that I did such-and-such yesterday, even though yesterday has already gone. It's not present. I can also imagine something about tomorrow. That's not real either, because tomorrow hasn't come yet. We're thinking about something that is not real right now, right here. This is a fabrication. To do zazen means to see this illusion for what it is, to understand that it is an illusion.

No matter what we think about it, we cannot be separated from the original self. We are universal whether we're alive or dead. At the same time, it's also true that we cannot be separated from our individual, personal self, either, which has the karma to produce all kinds of delusion. So we can conclude that the human condition involves existing in the midst of this relationship between personal self and universal self.

In our life as personal self, universal self is not something to yearn for, it is the direction toward which we should aim. This is the meaning of "vow." The first of the four bodhisattva vows is "Sentient beings are innumerable, I vow to save them all." This means to settle as universal life wherever that life naturally settles. The second vow is "Cravings are inexhaustible, I vow to extinguish them all." This means refraining from being dragged around by one's thoughts. But as long as we are human beings, we're going to have a mind that fabricates illusions, and so we have to continuously study the buddhadharma to clarify the reality of our self. This is the meaning of the third vow, "Dharma teachings are limitless, I vow to learn them all." The fourth vow is "The Buddha Way is endless, I vow to complete it." With this, we vow to settle as the universal self.

A classic Mahayana text says "The true mind of every sentient being itself teaches and leads each sentient being. This is the vow of Buddha."[65] Vow is not a special speculative approach to something outside ourselves. The true mind of sentient beings—that is, universal self—itself is vow. Thus, when we consider universal self from the vantage point of the personal self, we realize that we cannot live without vow.

On the other hand, when we consider personal self from the ground of universal self, we realize that we are not what we should be. We can't actualize universal self, because we are restrained by the handcuffs and fetters of karma. In this frame of mind, we can't help but repent. In the very nature of the relationship between universal self and personal self, vow and repentance naturally emerge. It's a mistake to consider it from only one perspective.

For example, Buddhist priests generally moralize too much. If we reflect upon ourselves intently, we can see that no one is entitled to do this. There's no use trying to hide the fact that none of us can carry out all our ethical teachings. When priests speak of moral issues, if we don't include our own faults in the form of repentance, it's just a kind of lie. I think this failure is why most people are unmoved by sermons. People listen to me without yawning, I guess, because when I talk about morality, I also reveal that I myself can't follow what I'm proposing. I try to expose my own faults as a form of repentance. And when I repent, the flame of my vow burns brighter. As humans committed to a life of zazen, we should maintain both attitudes, vow and repentance. These are our two practices.

You must grasp this: "One zazen, two practices, three minds." Don't try to find this expression in any sutra. It won't be there. I made it up. No Buddhist dictionary explains it yet. Someday it'll be there.

Anyway, the three minds—magnanimous mind, nurturing mind, and joyful mind—describe the way in which, as individual, personal selves, we should function to reveal our original, universal self.

I have already described magnanimous mind as the act of opening the hand of thought and refraining from any comparison or discrimination. For example, the word "big," which is written in Japanese with the same character as the "magnanimous" of "magnanimous mind," doesn't imply "bigger than something else." Anything only relatively big isn't really big, no matter what size it is.

I was amazed when I heard that there are researchers who study the genitals of fleas. Apparently they classify them according to their shape: some form an equilateral triangle, others an isosceles triangle, and still others are flat. They can tell from these distinguishing marks whether a certain flea lives on bears in Alaska, Siberia, or Hokkaido. Their research is very interesting. In any case, it seems that the genitals of fleas are proportionately quite big. I'll bet there are even parasitic microorganisms that live on the genitals of those fleas.

By contrast, if you send a satellite up into space, the Earth's landscape is blurry. Once I saw a photograph of Japan taken from such a satellite, and of course I couldn't see myself in the photograph. I could see Lake Biwa and Kyoto, so undoubtedly I was there, but because the picture was taken from orbit, I was smaller than a microorganism on a flea. Any time we compare the sizes of things in a *relative* way, we really can't tell which is big and which is small.

In Buddhism, "big" refers to something beyond comparison and differentiation. This is revealed when we open the hand of our thinking that discriminates between things. When we entirely let go of thought, magnanimous mind is there. Then we encounter everything as the all-inclusive self that is one with the ten directions *(jinjippō jinissai jiko)*. Wherever I find myself, I just live out the self that is nothing but the self, in my own way. This is magnanimous mind.

As a natural outgrowth of the attitude that whatever I encounter is nothing but myself, I take great care of my life. This is the approach toward everything that is called nurturing mind.

The love between lovers is different from conjugal affection. A marriage based exclusively on eros is bound to come to a sad end. Before marriage, there's no real need for the parties to serve one another. All they need is love. After marriage, when they start living together, romantic or erotic love alone isn't enough. Conjugal love between husband and wife requires each to think of the other first. Each one has to take care of the other.

This is important because often people are adults only physiologically; spiritually, they're still children. When childish people get married, it's only natural that they'll have trouble, because they expect others to take care of them. Only people who have matured and can take care of others have the nurturing mind of a loving parent. That is what maturity means: to meet others with nurturing mind. I realized this through my own mistakes, and I offer this as advice to every newly married couple.

In Buddhism this caring attitude is enlarged and applied to the whole world. In the Lotus Sutra, this is expressed in the verse:

In this triple world,
all is my domain;
The living beings in it
are all my children.

This is the mind that sympathizes with everything, that penetrates into everything—not for itself, but for others. As a natural extension, we need to find the real meaning of our life in taking care of others and in putting our life-spirit into that attitude and effort. To find our life worth living isn't the same thing as just feeling a constant emotional happiness. The life-spirit that meets everything with a nurturing mind is joyful mind.

We who are committed to a life of zazen must maintain the two practices of vow and repentance and the three minds in our zazen. An attitude of feeling safe and at peace as long as one is sitting is no good at all. All sentient beings are crying out in one form or another, they are suffering and in distress. We have to foster the vow deep in our hearts that we will work to settle all sentient beings. Vow is fundamental to our practice. Even though we take this vow, it is difficult to carry it out, so we have to acknowledge this about ourselves with a repentant heart. Then we have to actualize our vow through the functioning of the three minds.

4. Live by vow and root it deeply.

When I think of vow, I always remember the section on Bodhidharma in the essay called *Protecting and Maintaining Practice (Gyōji)* of Dōgen Zenji's *Shōbōgenzō*. *Gyōji* describes the purest and most concrete form of vow.

The First Ancestor in China came from the West as directed by Master Prajnatara. It took him three years to reach China by sea. He surely experienced innumerable hardships, including storms and blizzards, and faced great danger sailing on the wide ocean. Despite those difficulties, he managed to arrive in an unknown country. Ordinary people, who hold their lives dear, can't even imagine doing such a thing.

This way of protecting and maintaining practice [*gyōji*] stemmed from his great compassion and his vow to transmit the dharma and save deluded living beings. He was able to do it because he himself was the dharma-self of transmission and for him the whole universe was the world of transmitting dharma. He did it because he understood that the whole ten-direction world is nothing but self and that the whole ten-direction world is nothing but the whole ten-direction world.

Wherever you are living is a palace; and there is no palace that is not an appropriate place to practice the Way. This is why Bodhidharma came from the West the way he did. He had neither doubt nor fear, because he was living in the world of saving deluded living beings [the world of vow].

Creating the next generation has been my vow since I was a middle-school student, and becoming a Buddhist monk was one step in actualizing that vow. After I became a monk, the flame of my life blazed even brighter, despite the monastery buildings being terribly dilapidated and my life being very meager. When times were hard, I was encouraged and given strength most by that section of *Gyōji* in the *Shōbōgenzō,* describing Bodhidharma's life.

In those days my life was so wretched I felt as if I were being trampled, over and over again, the way we stamp on weeds, and I was never able to put forth even the tiniest bud. When things were tough, I chose to stick with my vow and bury it deeply in the earth to take root there. If I hadn't, that vow would have died, because I was always being trampled. But because the flame of that vow burned within me, the more I was beaten down, the deeper I rooted my vow to create the next generation.

I think it was the same for Bodhidharma. He made the huge effort to make the risky journey all the way from India to China, where he met Emperor Wu of Liang. The emperor couldn't understand the Indian monk, so Bodhidharma went to Mount Shaolin. In short, he was scorned. Still, he had vowed to transmit the dharma and save living beings. Because of that vow, he was able to live out his life. And while he was practicing zazen quietly at Mount Shaolin, he rooted the vow deeply in the ground.

Then Huike became his disciple. He, too, was trampled down his whole life, even after he became a disciple of Bodhidharma and practiced zazen. Through the times of the third, fourth, and fifth patriarchs, they all had a hard time, but they rooted themselves in their vows. By the time of the Sixth Patriarch, spring finally came and Zen started to ripen.

In my life, too, spring gradually arrived; quite a few people have gathered to follow in my footsteps either as lay practitioners or ordained disciples. Suppose that each of my disciples has his own disciples and that this were to continue for several centuries: it would be amazing, like a nuclear explosion!

This is not my selfish ambition, but my vow as buddhadharma: the vow to transmit the dharma and save deluded living beings, to live out life wherever, whenever, whatever happens. The self-of-the-whole-ten-direction-world grows by the action of the vow "Sentient beings are innumerable, I vow to save them all." This is why Dōgen Zenji said Bodhidharma could do what he did because he understood that this whole ten-direction world is nothing but the true Way, that this whole ten-direction world is nothing but self.

You have to expect to be trampled on by difficult circumstances, maybe even for many years, but don't lose your life force under all the pressure. Unless you have that vow, you will lose heart. Only when you live by vow does everything you meet—wherever, whenever, whatever happens—reinforce your life as buddhadharma. As long as you have that vow to live out your life wherever you are, sooner or later spring will come. And when it does, you will have the strength to grow. This is the life force. You have to thoroughly understand that this is completely different from selfish ambition.

Because I believe vow is so important, I made it a rule to chant only the four bodhisattva vows before and after my talks. There's no need to argue difficult philosophical matters. Just hold these four vows, they're essential.

5. Realizing that development and backsliding are your responsibility alone, endeavor to practice and develop.

There is a saying in Dōgen Zenji's *Instructions for the Cook (Tenzo Kyōkun)*, "A foolish person regards himself as another, a wise man regards others as himself."

Some people say we are living in the age of indifference. There are people who are as indifferent to themselves as they are to others. They are completely mixed up. Actually, there is no such thing as "other people." Other people are also your self, so "a wise man regards other people as himself." To live out your life as that self that is one with everything means that when you encounter other people, you should live out your self in that very meeting between you and them. Martin Buber spoke of "I and Thou." The self that meets other people as part of "I," he called by the name "Thou." What is most important here is the attitude of putting yourself in another's shoes.

Furthermore, you have to live out your self as your own responsibility. Ultimately, development and backsliding depend only on you. It really is pointless to say that you became rotten because of your circumstances, or that your education is responsible, or that the blame belongs to somebody else. The fundamental attitude of a practitioner must be to live out one's own whole self.[66]

You can spend your whole life oblivious of what's happening around you, or you can live your whole life with an aware mind. To live blindly is utterly meaningless. Bodhi-mind—or Way mind, or awakening mind—is that mind which constantly reminds you to wake up in the real sense. So, "realizing that development and backsliding are your responsibility alone, endeavor to practice and develop."

6. Sit silently for ten years, then for ten more years, and then for another ten years.

There is a saying, "One inch sitting—one inch buddha." It's silly to understand these words to mean that if you sit a little bit, you're a little bit of a buddha. "One inch sitting—one inch buddha" means that one inch is altogether buddha, so we should resolve to sit as much as possible.[67]

I've heard that in the Rinzai sect these days monks stay in the monasteries for only two or three years. In the Soto sect, it is even worse. Young people can receive qualification as a priest in as little as six months or a year, if they have a college degree from a good school, and then they leave monastic training. It really is nonsense. They just can't become true monks in two or three years.

We have to live out our self, understanding that everything depends on ourselves. We have to practice long enough to realize this attitude, sitting silently for at least ten years. When I became a monk, my father told me a proverb that says "Sit for three years, even on stone." So he told me to practice silently for three years. After three years had passed he said to me, "Bodhidharma sat facing the wall for nine years." And so I sat facing the wall for nine years.

But after ten years of practice, I made up my mind to practice ten more years. If you've been practicing for ten years, you can see just how long the next ten years will be. You begin to get it: "Aha! Ten years isn't so long." At first it seems that even a year or two of practice is too long and hard. But after ten years, it's not so difficult to make up your mind to practice for ten more.

"One inch sitting—one inch buddha" is true. *One inch sitting—* sitting for just a short time—is also good zazen, since there's no specific amount of time that we can say we should sit.

But the more we practice opening the hand of thought, the clearer it becomes to us that "self" is not the same as "thought." We come to see decisively that the true self is not something made up in our heads. True self is the self of everything, the self of the whole dharma world, the original self that is manifest when we let go of thought. In other words, if we practice for a long time, there really will be some result.

Even if we sit only for a short time, that is all right, there is no question that we become aware of reality in our sitting. Beginners' zazen and zazen after ten years of practice are not two different things. At the same time, I still maintain that it is essential to practice zazen continuously for a long time. Actually, we have to keep practicing our whole lives. To be aware of our true universal self, we should continue to practice as long as we live.

There is a chapter of the *Shōbōgenzō* titled *Refraining from All Evil (Shoaku Makusa)*. A passage in it says, "When all evil truly comes not-to-be-produced, the power of practice is completely actualized. This actualization embraces the whole earth, the whole world, all time, the whole dharma. The measure of its actualization can be found in the depth of refraining from evil."

Instead of just trying to avoid doing something evil by means of moral effort, we can actualize the universal self of the whole earth, the whole world, the whole dharma. In other words, when we settle in the universal self, all evil is necessarily not produced. "The measure of its actualization can be found in the depth of refraining [from evil]" means that when we keep on practicing zazen steadily, we will understand deeply that whenever, wherever, whatever happens, everything is universal. It is in that manner that all evil comes not-to-be-produced. That's why we have to practice as long as we live.

To spend your life being blinded and dragged around by your own desires is a pathetic thing. However you live, what you do with your life depends on you. With that understanding, just sit silently for ten years, then for another ten, and after that, for ten more years.

7. Cooperate with one another and aim to create a place where sincere practitioners can practice without trouble.

A place of practice is as important to the practitioner as soil is to the farmer. A good practice place must neither be a place for carrying on religious political intrigues, nor a place to try to clamber up the pseudo-spiritual ladder. To be practicing and to get caught up in sexual affairs, money, or fame—or even to be blinded by your own practice—is a terrible waste of time. There's an old saying, "The poor farmer makes weeds, the mediocre one makes crops, and the skilled farmer makes soil." I have spent my life trying to improve the soil, or practice-ground, where I practice, aiming to make Antaiji a place where sincere practitioners can live and work together with the least amount of trouble.

There's another side to this matter of cooperation. Sometimes people will cooperate with each other not only in working or in practicing zazen, but also in playing around and drinking. These things are not necessarily bad in and of themselves, but we have to be careful not to simply cooperate in diversion and delusion.

It is important that every one of us cooperate with each other, to protect and maintain an atmosphere conducive to practicing together. There is no one who can claim to always embody bodhi-mind, the mind that aspires to practice and attain enlightenment. Each of us gathers and contributes his or her own little bodhi-mind to the general effort. Sawaki Roshi often said that a monastery is like a charcoal fire in a hibachi. If you put in just one little coal, it will go out right away. But if you gather many small coals, each glowing just a little bit, then the fire will flare up. In the same way, every one of us should contribute a little bodhi-mind and thus enable our sangha to thrive.

Leaving Antaiji

The preceding seven points cover the things I kept before me all the time I was abbot of Antaiji. I hope they will serve you as a point of reference. I wrote a poem about where I am now, though I am not sure whether it really qualifies as a poem or not.

> As an old man
> I have my own practice.
> It is different from that of youth.
> It is not working facing outward,
> but just facing inward, gazing at myself.
> And like the clouds that disappear
> into the expansive sky
> I, too, will disappear quietly.

Lately, I have fully realized that when we open the hand of thought, we are the self of the whole dharma world whether we think so or not.

Do you understand this self of the whole dharma world? Everything is one with everything, whether we think so or not. That is our true self. Perhaps you don't believe it, but the reality of it continues anyway. If we open the hand of thought, we are one with the whole universe. This truth leads to the crucial point for us of what role we should be playing right now, right here.

While Sawaki Roshi was alive, my role was that of a novice monk. I played that role for a pretty long time. I was a novice until I was fifty-two or fifty-three years old. Even though I was a novice, I was already an old monk. I played the role of the old novice right up to the end.

After Sawaki Roshi passed away I took on a new role, that of an abbot. Giving talks and being a teacher have been part of my role. I have spent all my effort at fulfilling that role.

Then my role became that of retiring. It would be silly to think that being a novice was no good, being an abbot was good, and that going into retirement was becoming worthless again. People too often think that way. But it isn't true. I think the most important thing is our attitude toward each role, devoting ourselves to it entirely. An old priest counseled me not to retire. He said that once you retire all your power gets taken away by your disciples. Personally, I don't think that way at all. It's just another role.

When I became abbot I declared that I would retire after ten years, because the population of old people is increasing in Japan. If old people do not retire to make way for the younger generation, there is going to be trouble, so I wanted to set an example.

We shouldn't imagine that life after retirement has to be miserable or impoverished. To be old is also one of our roles. When we're young, our role is to work; upon retirement, we take up another role. Since we have less income, we should simplify our lives as much as possible. That is the way to fulfill the role of an old person. We should not judge it miserable, but just devote ourselves to that particular role. We function through our roles and exert ourselves in our occupations as a role. Finally, dying is one of our roles.

I wrote another poem about this:

This "I" is the self of the whole dharma world
whether I think so or not.
This self of the whole dharma world
fulfills the role of life when in life,

and the role of death when in death.

Life is the manifestation of one's entire self.

Death is the manifestation of one's whole self.

As I said before, we don't actually live and die in our thoughts. When we are alive, life is the whole—all is alive. When we are dead, death is the whole—all is death. When we are alive, the entirety of life beyond thought is living. When we die, all of life including thought will die. When we are alive, the self-of-the-whole-dharma-world is in the role of life. Then, when we die, the self-of-the-whole-dharma-world is in the role of death. This is the meaning of "Life is the manifestation of one's entire self. / Death is the manifestation of one's whole self." After I retired, being retired became a manifestation of my whole self.

When I announced my retirement, the mother of one of my disciples visited me and she, too, said, "You're retiring too young." But I disagree. When I became the abbot after Sawaki Roshi's death, that gave me the role of teacher. So I devoted myself to fulfilling that role. I don't think you should be a teacher for too long. You can be a good teacher only in the beginning, because you're filled with the passion to educate. After a time, even if your technique has improved, you lose that passion. The passion to teach is more essential than any teaching technique.

The students you teach when you are a young schoolteacher will remember you and come to visit you in later years. But the students you teach as you get older do not visit you after they graduate. The students you taught when you first began teaching, when you had that passion to educate but no technique, are the ones who miss you.

Some people asked, "Since you're retiring so young, does that mean you are planning to control things at Antaiji after you retire?" They were referring to the practice of some of the early emperors of Japan, who actually interfered and controlled the government more after their retirement; it seems as if they retired especially in order to devote themselves to power. I have no desire whatever to do that. Seeing retirement as a role in itself, I have to die completely to active service. I know I will probably have to be taken care of by my disciples, because I am getting old, but I have no wish to interfere with them. I have decided to die completely to that kind of life and will lie happily in the shadow of the grass—that is, in the grave—knowing you're all practicing sincerely. I will lie there sorrowing if you live blindly. Please let me lie cheerfully in the shadow of the grass. I ask this of you wholeheartedly.

Opening

the

Hand

of

Thought

—

172

Notes

Preface

1. In the preface to *Jiko,* Uchiyama quotes from Eihei Dōgen Zenji to the effect that, while living a life of basic subsistence, we should strive to live out the highest culture.
2. "Ultimate refuge" is a translation of the Buddhist term *hikkyōki.* *Hikkyō* means "ultimate" or "absolute," while *ki* refers to "place of arrival." In his *Bukkyō Daijiten,* Nakamura Hajime defines this term as meaning *satori,* or "to go to the end." In the chapter *Hotsubodaishin* ("Awakening the Mind of Enlightenment") of Dōgen's *Shōbōgenzō* there is a passage "*Hikkyō* is the ultimate fruit of the Buddha [embodied] in the bodhisattva."

Chapter 1: Practice and Persimmons

3. Romans 7:9.
4. According to Nakamura Hajime, the *sanbōin,* the three seals, do not appear in the Pali Canon, but they do appear later, in the Chinese version. Traditionally, the three seals are *shogyō mujō,* all things are impermanent; *shohō muga,* all things are without a substantial self, and *nehan jakujō,* nirvana is peace prior to both movement and stillness. *Sangai kaiku,* all things in the three worlds (of past, present, and future) are suffering, is sometimes listed as the

fourth seal, while other scholars seem to feel that *shohō jissō,* all things are as they are, is the fourth seal.

5. Uchiyama Roshi writes about the definition of suffering in chapter 5 of *Kannon-gyō wo Ajiwau* ("Appreciating the Sutra of Kannon Bosatsu," subtitled "The Practice of the East," published by Hakujusha, Tokyo, 1968): "Though we can never be fully aware of all the suffering in the world, we should call out the name Kanzeon Bosatsu with our whole spirit in order that we may take on (be one with) that suffering." When I sense that immensity of suffering, then as if out of deepest grief, I cannot help but utter "Kanzeon Bosatsu" with all my heart. In other words, uttering "Namu Kanzeon Bosatsu" should not simply come out of our being troubled with some petty thing in our lives. We have to cry out "Kanzeon Bosatsu" as our practice day and night, regardless of whether we are capable of penetrating the depth of that suffering or not.

6. In this discussion, there is no inner world separate from an outer world. For Uchiyama, he is the creator of everything he knows or is, everything in his world, including what appears "outside." Creating one's world implies nurturing an awareness of that world. In the *Abhidharma-kosa* (Jp., *Kusharon*), for example, this idea is explained in the concept of *jiko,* where "self" is used inclusive of "other."

7. *Kū* is written with the character that also means *sky* (Jp., *sora*). The term derives from the Sanskrit terms *akasa,* which is vast, all-pervasive space, and *sunyata,* or emptiness.

8. Sawaki Roshi said in his lectures on Dōgen's *Gakudō Yōjinshū (Points to Watch in Practicing the Buddha Way),* "I've had several big satoris and numerous small ones, and I can tell you that it doesn't amount to a hill of beans."

Chapter 2: The Meaning of Zazen

9. "The reality of your own true self" is Uchiyama Roshi's way of expressing the Buddhist term *sarva-dharma-tathata* or *shohō jissō,* which first appeared in the Lotus Sutra. Originally, *shohō jissō* was a purely nominative expression that could be translated as the true form (reality) of all phenomena. Later on, the Chinese Tendai teaching interpreted the phrase in a predicative way that could be translated as "all phenomena are nothing but reality"—that is, the temporary existence of all things, though having no independent nature,

is a manifestation of reality. In Zen, both of these interpretations of the original Sanskrit felt too abstract, so the expression arose "our original face is the true form of all things." It is this undeniable truth, *shohō jissō,* that lies behind Roshi's colloquial expressions "the reality of one's true self" and "the reality of life."

10. Kōdō Sawaki's original expression *jiko ga jiko o jiko suru,* "zazen is the self doing itself by itself," is his colloquial way of expressing Dōgen's *jijuyū zanmai,* or the samadhi of freely receiving and giving, or utilizing. This might also be translated as "Zazen is the self making the self into the self." The original expression uses "self" as the subject, verb, and object.

11. In this case, "others" refers not only to people, but to things and concepts as well—in other words, anything outside of self.

12. "The very quick of life" is Uchiyama's term *nama no inochi,* literally "fresh, raw life." A fish swimming in a stream is alive and fresh, but once it is caught it gets processed. In the same way, all the terms we use to discuss universal self are a sort of processing or categorizing of what is always alive, fresh, and unprocessable.

13. All of these are interpretive renderings of various Japanized-Sanskrit terms. *Tathata* has been variously translated as suchness, the reality of things as they are, as-it-isness. Emptiness of reality is a translation of *nyo-jitsu-kū;* reality as it truly is beyond reasoning is *rigen shinnyo;* inexpressible *tathata* is *haisen shinnyo;* and true emptiness is *shinkū.* The first two expressions appear in the *Awakening of Mahayana Faith (Daijō Kishinron),* while the latter expressions appear in *The Great Wisdom Discourse (Daichidoron),* a commentary on the *Maha Prajna Paramita Sutra,* attributed to Nagarjuna.

14. It is said that a person knows cold things and warm things only when they are personally experienced. This comes from the expression *reidan jichi,* which literally means "heat and cold—only oneself knows."

15. Here, when Uchiyama says "the real life-experience of self," he uses the expression *seimei taiken.* This is in contrast to *seikatsu keiken,* which refers to each individual's experiences in life. Life-experience means that life exists as what we experience prior to coloration of our thoughts of suffering or happiness. The significance of this is that a person who has a happy experience will tend to interpret the world in a bright way, while someone who has a painful experience will interpret the world as being dark. Here, life-experience precedes the coloration of pleasure or pain; this means self cannot be separated

from world (that which is experienced)—self and world are one reality. Practice as life-experience actualizes life—self and world—as one reality.

16. The Japanese expression translated as "Japanese spirituality" is *nihonteki rei-sei*. D. T. Suzuki used this expression as the title for a book he wrote in 1944 (Daitō Publishers). In brief, he defines spirituality as follows: Spirituality is that which transcends the dichotomy of spiritual and material (phenomena or world). Spirituality is the foundation of spirit (mind) and material. Spirit and material are not one, but not two, either. Spiritual intuition enables us to see that reality. He says further that this spirituality is, at the same time, religious consciousness. He explains the Japanese way of manifesting this spirituality through Zen and Pure Land Buddhism.

Chapter 3: The Reality of Zazen

17. Traditionally, sitting cross-legged in full-lotus posture, *kekkafuza* in Japanese, or in the half-lotus, *hankafuza,* has been considered very important. They are the most helpful positions, because sitting cross-legged with knees and buttocks creating a stable tripod makes it much easier to sit upright with the pelvis tipped, which in turn makes it easier for your breath to settle in your belly (more precisely, in the *tanden;* see note 18) and thus it is much easier to maintain your whole zazen posture. So it is well worth trying to teach your body to sit cross-legged—if you can. Other arrangements are not "wrong," they are just more difficult for maintaining an attitude of aiming at zazen posture. Some people sit in a kneeling position on a zabuton (*seiza* posture), resting their buttocks on a low bench or an up-ended zafu. You can sit zazen in a chair or on a stool, too. Make sure your feet rest securely on the floor, use a low wedge cushion to tip your pelvis slightly, and if needed use lower back support so your muscles are not straining to hold your torso upright, but do not lean backwards.

18. The area about two inches below the navel is called the *tanden* or *hara*. If you are maintaining the correct zazen posture, the center of gravity of your body and mind will naturally fall to the *tanden*. When you breathe during zazen, the center of gravity should fall to the *tanden* by means of maintaining the correct posture. Other than that, just breathe naturally.

Uchiyama pointed out a passage on breath in the *Eihei Kōroku* (vol. 5), a collection of sermons by Dōgen Zenji, which says:

In our zazen, it is of primary importance to sit in the correct posture. Next, regulate the breath and calm down. For hinayana practitioners, there are two elementary ways [of beginning practice]: one is to count breaths, and the other is to contemplate the impurity [of the body]. In other words, a practitioner with a hinayana [attitude] regulates his breathing by counting his breaths. However, the practice of the buddha—-patriarchs is completely different from the way of hinayana. A patriarch has said, "It is better to have the mind of a wily fox than to follow the hinayana way of self-regulation." Two of the hinayana schools [studied] in Japan today are the Shibunritsu and Kusha schools.

There is also a Mahayana way of regulating the breath. That is, knowing that a long breath is long and that a short one is short. The breath reaches the tanden and returns from there. Although the exhalation and inhalation are different, they both pass through the tanden. When you breathe abdominally, it is easy to become aware of the transiency (of life), and to regulate the mind.

My former teacher Rujing said: "The inhaled breath reaches the tanden; however, it isn't that this breath comes from somewhere. For this reason, it is neither long nor short. The breath goes out from the tanden, but it is not a matter of it going somewhere. For that reason, it is neither short nor long."

My teacher explained it in that way, and if someone were to ask me how to regulate the breath, I would reply in this way. Although it is not Mahayana [as some fixed doctrine], it is different from hinayana; though it is not hinayana, it is different from Mahayana. And, if questioned further regarding what it is ultimately, I would respond that inhaling or exhaling are neither long nor short.

19. For example, in our calculating mind, when we divide 10 by 3 we always get a remainder. In trying to understand or explain zazen, no matter how deeply or from how many angles we approach it, there is always going to remain an area that cannot be solved by intellectual calculation. We are told to aim at holding the posture of zazen, yet the aiming is an action without any goal. Behind this word "indefinite" is also the realization of how petty and powerless this small ego-centered self actually is.

20. In the *Shōbōgenzō: Genjō Kōan,* Dōgen writes about this point, that there is no reason to think we will perceive it when we actualize reality: "When buddhas are truly buddhas, there is no perception of oneself as being buddha," and, in the *Shōbōgenzō: Bendōwa,* he says, "However, such things do not come into the perceptions of the person sitting, because they take place in the

stillness of samadhi, without any fabrication, and constitute enlightenment itself."

21.   [Uchiyama Roshi's note on shikantaza—just sitting] The aim of doing zazen is to do zazen. It is never doing zazen for another purpose, such as gaining some sort of special enlightenment. I believe the following passages from Dōgen elucidate this point:

"Zazen itself is satori. Zazen is dropping off body and mind and is the Shōbōgenzō-nehanmyōshin [the spiritual wisdom of the true dharma]. Doing zazen is to practice, put into effect, and actualize this satori—here-and-now. Only when we do zazen with this attitude can our practice of zazen be called shikantaza—just doing." *(Shōbōgenzō: Zanmai ō Zanmai)*

In the preceding passage Dōgen Zenji is being quite clear in stating that satori is not so-called enlightenment. Nor is it some special experience one strives for by doing zazen.

"The correctly transmitted dharma from buddha to buddha and from patriarch to patriarch has always been just to sit.... This is very clear. Zazen itself is already the ultimate posture of satori. In other words, satori is just doing zazen." (*Eihei Kōroku,* vol. 4)

"The way that has been transmitted from buddha to buddha and from patriarch to patriarch is to practice the Way doing zazen. Tiantong Rujing [Tendō Nyōjō, Dōgen's teacher] said, 'Sitting with folded legs is the posture of the ancient buddhas. Therefore, entrusting the body to sanzen [Translators' note: Literally, giving up to Zen; in the Shōbōgenzō: Zazengi, Dōgen states unambiguously that sanzen is zazen} is dropping off body and mind. Burning incense (to settle the mind), reverent bowing before Buddha images, reciting the nembutsu (repetition of the Buddha's name), special practices of repenting, reading the sutras, and other religious ceremonies are unnecessary. It is enough just to do zazen.'" (*Eihei Kōroku,* vol. 6)

"When Bodhidharma came to China, he didn't engage himself in all sorts of so-called religious practices. Nor did he give lectures on the sutras. He simply did zazen at Shōrinji for nine years just facing the wall. Doing zazen, just that, is the way of the buddhas, the shōbōgenzō nehanmyōshin." (*Eihei Kōroku,* vol. 4)

"My late teacher Tiantong Rujing [Tendō Nyojō] said: "Practicing zazen is dropping off body and mind. You can attain this through the practice of shikantaza alone. The practices of incense burning, bowing, visualizing, or chanting the nembutsu, repentance, or reading the sutras are unnecessary." In the last several hundred years, it was my late teacher alone who gouged out the eyes of the buddhas and patriarchs and sat therein. Few people have clarified that sitting is the buddhadharma, that the buddhadharma is sitting. Even though some have understood through experience that sitting is the buddhadharma, none have known that sitting is just sitting. Much less have there been any who have held that the buddhadharma is just the buddha-dharma." *(Shōbōgenzō: Zanmai ō Zanmai)* [Translators: The eye is a metaphor for wisdom, and this passage describes Dōgen's teacher's ability to sit in the buddhas' and ancestors' place and to see through their eyes.]

22. Uchiyama Roshi coined his own rather unusual but colloquial expression for letting go of thoughts: *omoi no tebanashi,* literally, "releasing your grip on thoughts." In the Buddhist sense, the word *omoi* includes not only thoughts and ideas, but all feelings and emotions as well.

23. The following dialogue (Jp., *mondō*) is a famous source of the expression "thought of no thought." It took place between the Chinese master Yaoshan Weiyan (Jp., Yakusan Igen, 751–834 c.e.), and one of his disciples.

When Yaoshan was sitting, a monk asked him: "What do you think when you sit?" The Master said, "I think of not thinking." The monk queried further, "How do you think of not thinking?" Yaoshan replied, "[By sitting] beyond thinking."

When we are sitting, we do not follow our thoughts, nor do we stop them. We just let them come and go freely. We cannot call it thinking, because the thoughts are not grasped. If we simply follow our thinking, it is exactly that, and not zazen. We cannot call it not thinking, either, because thoughts are coming and going, like clouds floating in the sky. When we are sitting, our brains don't stop working, just as our stomachs don't stop digesting. Sometimes our minds are busy; sometimes they are calm. Just sitting without being concerned with the condition of our minds is the most important point of zazen.

24. The Chinese characters for Keizan's expression *kakusoku* literally mean to awaken and touch. The expression is used to imply living life more fully and alive.

25. In this case, "actualize" is not being used in the sense of putting some potential into operation, but rather means to allow the functioning of that which is always being manifested.

26. Yongjia Xuanjue (Jp., Yōka Genkaku) was a seventh-century Chinese master. The "five elements of existence," or *skandhas* (Skt.), are body, feeling, percep-

tion, volition, and consciousness. These are literally "heaps" or "aggregations" of characteristics that in sum make up what we provisionally call a "person." The "three poisons"—greed, hatred or anger, and delusion or ignorance— are the three primary unwholesome conditions, or roots, of our ethics and actions. There are three corresponding positive roots. "Hellish destiny" is a poetic rendering of "avici karma," actions that send us spiraling downward to hell realms, which are the three lower forms of existence in the traditional six-realm wheel of life.

[Uchiyama Roshi's note follows.] It also says in the Shōdōka, "Neither try to eliminate delusion, nor seek after what is real. The true nature of ignorance, just as it is, is buddha-nature. The body itself, which appears and disappears like a phantom, is nothing other than the dharma-body (reality of life). Waking up to the reality of life, there is no particular thing we can point to and say, 'This is it.'"

27. Here Nagarjuna is criticizing an attitude on the part of the practitioner who seeks only to control his own mind and emotions (pratyeka buddha) and tries to escape from the world (shravaka)—or, to put it another way, to escape from the provisional subject-object world.

28. Hinayana is a term that was used pejoratively by early Buddhists, including Dōgen Zenji, to refer to people who, although they claimed to be Buddhists, were actually wrapped up only in their own salvation, which they understood to have no connection to other sentient beings. In other words, they lacked a vision that would include all people. As a term, hinayana would seem to be the opposite of mahayana, but to understand it in such a way is a mistake. Hinayana never properly referred to a school, only to a narrow attitude.

It should follow from this that the term mahayana, too, although sometimes used to indicate a school of Buddhism, is also being used pejoratively by Dōgen when referring to Buddhists who have become attached to the term. Readers of Buddhist texts, especially those of Dōgen, must be careful in discerning whether he is using a term to designate a school or whether he is talking about an attitude.

29. That is, seeking nirvana becomes the cause of further suffering.

30. The word translated here as "fogged over" is bokeru in Japanese. "Fogged over" is meant to cover both extremes of how our lives become unclear or muddled—that is, by frenetic activity or busyness (chasing after every whim or desire) and through sluggish activity (like laziness).

31. When Uchiyama uses the expression "foundation of life," he does so in contrast to a shallow or dualistic way of living based on existence, or survival, mentality.

32. When Uchiyama says "our whole world turns into anger," he is explaining the Japanese Buddhist expression *wakugokku,* roughly "grasping onto ignorance." Sawaki often explained this concept in the following way: Thoughts are fantasies, acts are real, and the results come back to haunt us.

33. In the *Shōbōgenzō: Zazenshin,* Dōgen has the expression *tori tonde tori ni nitari*—"the flying bird resembles a bird." That is, there is no real substance to all of the "things" to which we attach names. That which has no form (the flying bird) here and now takes a temporary form of a bird (resembles a bird). Dōgen's expression is his way of phrasing Nagarjuna's "Seeing the arisal of various dharmas [things] destroys the view that nothing exists substantially. Seeing the decay of various dharmas destroys the view that things exist substantially. For this reason, although all the dharmas appear to exist, they are like phantoms, like dreams" (From the *Mula-madhyamaka-sastra* of Nagarjuna, *Commentary on the Middle Way;* in Jp., *Chūron*).

34. [Uchiyama's note] Zazen is the practice of the Buddha. Zazen is nondoing. This is indeed our genuine self. As buddhadharma, nothing else is to be sought after [Dōgen, *Shōbōgenzō: Zuimonki*].

Chapter 4: The World of Intensive Practice

35. Literally, the word *sesshin* means to touch or listen to one's true mind. There are two different Chinese characters for the first syllable in *sesshin,* both of which are read *setsu.* One means to touch, the other means to listen to. The second character, *shin,* which is translated literally as "mind," might better be understood to mean "life," or at least something broader than merely psychological mind, as that would make little sense in the context of Uchiyama's discussion of universal self.

   Life in any Zen monastery or center includes periodic sesshins. Traditionally, the practice of sesshin, which consists of specified periods of three days, five days, a week, or a month or more devoted to zazen, is an important part of the formal contemplative aspect of Zen practice.

36. Uchiyama's expression translated as "self which is only self" is *jiko giri no jiko.* Even in Japanese, this is not an ordinary expression and can be understood best by carefully considering the examples Uchiyama uses to explain

this absolute aspect of self. This is the true self that is just itself, naked, not wobbling about relative to others and full of desires, but settled in itself. Uchiyama quotes from Sawaki about how it is impossible to exchange so much as a fart with another person to explain in down-to-earth language the meaning of "self which is only self."

37. Time is a human fabrication. A minute and an hour are human standards that have been established to "measure" the "flowing swiftness" labeled time. That only five minutes have passed, or that it *feels like* an hour has passed, is due to our having fixed a relative label—time—and invested a value in this fixed standard, such as "time is money." However, if we let go of this comparative standard, time does not exist as any such fixed entity.

38. That sesshin continues "as it is" is a translation of the expression *kaku no gotoku,* with the same meaning as *nyoze,* indicating that the sesshin continues regardless of the fiction of time.

39. The point here is to remove any idea the sitter might embrace about having stuck it out through the five days by virtue of his own individual strength.

40. "The bottom of our thoughts...falls out" is a paraphrase of the Zen expression *taha shittsū,* which appears in the *Blue Cliff Record* (Jp., *Hekigan-roku).*

41. The "scenery of our zazen" means the appearance of the world as seen, heard, felt, and so on, through our senses.

Chapter 5: Zazen and the True Self

42. When Uchiyama has the squashes say, "We're all tied together and living just one life," the word "one" in the expression "one life" is used in an absolute, noncomparative sense. It does not mean one little lifetime among many. The drawings in figures 12–14 are by Uchiyana Roshi.

43. There is a linguistic problem here that needs some explanation. What we have translated as "zazen...enables us to wake up" can also be read "zazen makes us wake up." "Enables" seems closer to the spirit of Dōgen than "forces" or "makes." In Japanese, the form of the verb used to indicate command or force can also be used to indicate permission: to allow, permit, or enable. Consequently, whether we are *made* to wake up or *enabled* to wake up depends on the attitude of the sitter, since both the thoughts of "wanting to let go of thoughts" and "not wanting to let go" arise and cease of themselves.

The Japanese expression translated here as "the undivided reality of life that pervades the whole universe" is *jinissai butsuzuki no seimei.* It is a combination of Dōgen's *jinissai,* which implies all-pervading, and Uchiyama's *butsuzuki no seimei,* undivided life.

44. The Japanese expressions in this passage are *honrai no jiko,* "one's original self"; *jinjippōkai-jiko,* "the self that pervades the ten-direction world"; *jindai-chi-jiko,* "the self that fills the whole earth"; and *jinissai-jiko,* "universal self."

45. In Japanese, "all living things" is *issai seimei,* while "everything that exists" is *issai sonzai.* These expressions are Uchiyama's translations of two old Japanese expressions, *ikitoshi ikeru mono,* "all living things," and *arito arayu-ru mono,* "all existing things."

46. Zazen that is the activity of the reality of life is, as used by Dōgen, *shōjō no shu. Shō,* sometimes translated as "enlightenment," actually means "reality." Since we are living the reality of the life of universal self, we practice or actualize the reality of this life through zazen. It is sometimes translated as "practice beyond enlightenment," or "practice based on enlightenment." Either translation implies that Dōgen is suggesting that we first have to gain enlightenment, and then we can practice. However, this is not what he meant. Practice based on or beyond enlightenment simply means practice that precedes any concept of either enlightenment or delusion. He also expresses this idea through the expressions *shushō ichinyo,* "practice and enlightenment are one," and *honshō myōshu,* "true practice is a manifestation of original enlightenment."

47. The Sanskrit Buddhist word is *sraddha,* defined in the Indian Abhidharma-kosa, an early scholastic text that defines many Buddhist terms, as clarity or purity; it is also often translated as confidence in the dharma or self-confidence in the sense of universal self.

   [Uchiyama Roshi's note] In the *Commentary on the Awakening of Mahayana Faith* (Jp., *Daijōkishinron-giki*) the Buddha's vow is described as follows: "The true mind of the sentient being turns around and awakens the sentient being himself.... In other words, this true mind itself is the Buddha's vow of compassion." Since we are already living out life connected to all things, we are awakened and led by that life. Buddhism expresses this fact by saying that the Buddha saves sentient beings by means of vows. Therefore, you should understand that even if I talk about the vow of Amitabha, I am not talking about some other person or thing called Amitabha. Amitabha is not outside of the self.

48. This appears in the Maha-prajna-paramita-shastra, *Commentary on the Great Perfection of Wisdom.*

49. [Uchiyama Roshi's note] The following is a list of just a few of the more commonplace expressions that have been used to express universal self: *shinnyo* (Skt., *tathata;* Eng., suchness); *hosshō* (Skt., *dharmata;* Eng., dharma-nature); *hosshin* (Skt., *dharmakaya;* Eng., dharma body); *hokkai* (Skt., *dharmadhatu;* Eng., dharma world); *busshō* (Skt., *buddhata;* Eng., buddha-nature); *nyoraizō* (Skt., *tathagata-garbha;* Eng., matrix, womb, or embryo of tathagata); *shin* (Skt., *hridaya;* Eng., mind); *yuishin* (Skt., *citta-matra;* Eng., mind-only); *isshin* (Skt., *svacitta-matra;* Eng., one mind); *funi* (Skt., *advaita;* Eng., nonduality); *ichijō* (Skt., *ekayana;* Eng., one or single vehicle); *jissō* (Skt., *tathata;* Eng., all things are as they are); *myō* (Skt., *sunyata;* Eng., emptiness); *hikkyōku* (Skt., *atyanta-sunyata;* Eng., ultimately empty); *nyonyo* (Skt., *tathata;* Eng., suchness); *nyozehō* (Skt., *yatha-dharma;* Eng., in accordance with the law); *nehan* (Skt., *nirvana;* Eng., nirvana); *hiu himu* (Skt., *na bhavo napi cabhavah;* Eng., not-existing, not-not-existing); *chudō* (Skt., *madhyana-pratipad;* Eng., Middle Way); *daiichi gitai* (Skt., *parainartha;* Eng., absolute truth).

50. "All-encompassing self," *jinissai jiko,* can be found in the *Shōbōgenzō: Yuibutsu Yobutsu (Only Buddha Together with Buddha).*

51. The point of these expressions of "life actualizes life" and "buddha actualizes buddha" is to cut through the idea of doing zazen for any other reason than for its own sake. They are expressions reflecting the same point as *jiyuyū zanmai,* that there is nothing outside of self. The subject, the action, and the object of our lives is our self. This expression is difficult to understand not because of translation difficulties in rendering the original Japanese into English, but due to the difficulty of expressing the buddhadharma in words.

52. Dōgen went to China in 1223 and, after visiting various teachers, finally practiced under Rujing. The records of the teaching he received from Rujing are called the *Hōkyōki.* The following is from the *Hōkyōki.*

"Rujing addressed the monks, 'Sanzen is dropping off body and mind. Without employing the burning of incense, services, rituals, or the chanting of sutras and the special practices of *nembutsu,* or repentance, just do *shikantaza* (zazen).'

Dōgen asked, 'What is dropping off body and mind?'

Rujing replied, 'Dropping off body and mind is zazen!'"

In other words, to give yourself up unconditionally to zazen—to surrender to zazen—is dropping off body and mind. Dropping off body and mind is to really sit zazen. So it's not a matter of gradually dropping off our body and mind by means of zazen. Zazen itself is the reality of dropping off body and mind. Sitting, practicing, and putting our faith in zazen is dropping off body and mind. In other words, *satori* means to realize that practice is satori; satori is not something we gain gradually as the result of practice. This certainly becomes clear in the quotation just given. This attitude is called *shōjō no shu,* "the activity of the reality of life," or *shushō ichinyo,* "the identity of activity and the reality of life."

Chapter 6: The World of Self Unfolds

53. In Dōgen's *Shōbōgenzō: Kōmyō (Glorious Brightness)* is the following passage: "The light of the buddha-patriarchs is the whole-ten-direction-universe, all the buddhas, all the patriarchs, buddha and buddha; it is the light of buddha, the light is buddha. The buddha-patriarchs lighten the buddha-patriarchs. The buddha-patriarchs practice and realize this light; they become buddha, sit buddha, and actualize buddha."

54. The Middle Way is called that because it is the way of the center, of truth, avoiding the false extremes of nihilism on one hand, the view that nothing is real or worthwhile; and substantialism on the other hand, the view that things exist permanently and that people have permanent souls.

55. This passage appears in the *Samyutta Nikaya.* It is translated here from the Japanese edition of the Tripitaka, which is the complete traditional Buddhist canon. (*Taishō Shinshū Daizō-kyō, Zoagon-kyō,* pp. 301, 262.)

56. In Buddhism, ignorance (Jp., *mumyō*; Skt., *avidya*) is defined as being in the dark about truth. The Chinese characters literally mean "without light." Ignorance is understood to be one of the most fundamental factors in human suffering.

57. Many of Uchiyama's expressions can be traced back to the twelvefold chain of interdependence, sometimes referred to as the twelve links of causation, or sometimes a shorter list of five links of dependent origination. The first of the twelve links was originally said to be ignorance.

58. Uchiyama's lifelong interest in Christianity spilled over in his explanations of Buddhist teachings. He frequently pointed out parallels in the two religions.

Chapter 7: Living Wide Awake

59. There are many definitions of "bodhisattva." *Bodhi* is enlightenment or being awake, and *sattva* is a being, so the word literally means "awakening being" or "enlightening being." Most schools of Buddhist thought would agree on defining a bodhisattva as a person who seeks to practice the Way of the Buddha, sometimes referred to as a Wayseeker. In the Mahayana teachings this has been interpreted to mean one who practices for the benefit of all beings.

60. Uchiyama's commentary on the three minds, along with a translation of the *Tenzo Kyōkun*, is published in English as *From the Zen Kitchen to Enlightenment* (originally titled *Refining Your Life*, translated by Tom Wright (Tokyo, Weatherhill, 1983). It was published in Japanese as *Jinsei Ryōri no Hon—Tenzo Kyōkun ni Manabu* by Sōtōshū Shūmuchō, 1970. The *Chiji Shingi* chapter of the *Eihei Daishingi* was published by Hakujusha Publishers under the title *Seimei no Hataraki—Chiji Shingi o Ajiwau (The Function of Life—Appreciating the Chiji Shingi)*, 1972.

Chapter 8: The Wayseeker

61. The original Japanese expression for "group stupidity" is *gurupu boke.* Sawaki Roshi talked at length about this in various lectures. By *group stupidity* is meant a sort of mental paralysis of the individual to use sound judgment and being dragged around by the power of the group or society. *Boke* is the noun form of the verb *bokeru,* which includes both a sense of forgetting and of growing senile.

62. *Shosho gedatsu* literally refers to emancipation here and there, while *betsubetsu gedatsu* refers to emancipation gained by upholding particular precepts. Upholding each particular precept brings the benefit (emancipation) from upholding that precept. For example, if one vows not to kill any living thing and is able to uphold that precept, then the benefit of not killing will accrue.

63. This quotation can be found in Dōgen's *Gakudō Yōjinshū (Points to Watch in Practicing the Way).*

64. "Conditioned self" is a translation of *seirai no jibun,* while "original self" comes from *honrai no jiko.* Conditioned self is also referred to as karmic self.

65. This comes from the *Commentary on 'The Awakening of Faith'* (Ch., *Ta-ch'eng ch'i-hsin lun;* Jp., *Daijōkishinron-giki*) written by the great Chinese Buddhist master Fatsang (Fazang; Jp., Hōzō; 643–712).

66. The phrase used here, "one's whole self" is a loose translation of the Japanese *zenki,* which means "the whole function" or "the whole workings." It is also the title of a chapter in Dōgen's *Shōbōgenzō.*

67. Common sense tells us one inch is a little bit, but "one inch sitting—one inch buddha" cuts through our ideas of measuring and counting. It means that comparison is irrelevant, so we should throw away our comparing mind and sit knowing that the wholehearted sitting of a beginner is as much buddha as the wholehearted sitting of the most seasoned practitioner.

Glossary

Agamas and Nikayas: Among the earliest Buddhist teachings.

ancestors: A term for Zen predecessors, it is used in place of "patriarchs," and is often coupled with "buddhas," as in the phrase "buddhas and ancestors."

Antaiji: Established in the northern outskirts of Kyoto early in this century as a research center for Eihei Dōgen Zenji's works, particularly the *Shōbōgenzō*. Abbots Kōdō Sawaki Roshi and Kōshō Uchiyama Roshi retained the research aspect of the temple, but also formed it into a practice center. From the late 1960s through the mid-1970s, Antaiji drew practitioners from all around the world. All the abbots of Antaiji resisted pressures for the temple to become an official training monastery, in order to stay out of the limelight. With Uchiyama Roshi's retirement, the succeeding abbot moved Antaiji out of Kyoto and into the mountains. The number of practitioners dropped drastically and, at present, the temple has only about a half dozen residents.

Bodhidharma (Jp., *Bodaidaruma*): The founder and first ancestor of Zen in China, early in the sixth century. An Indian, he traveled to China, where he propagated Zen by sitting in a cave above Shao-lin-ssu (in Japanese, Shōrinji).

bodhisattva (Jp., *bodaisatta* or *bosatsu*): Anyone who seeks enlightenment through vows to save all sentient beings.

buddhadharma: In a narrow sense, the teachings of Shakyamuni Buddha and his successors. In a broader sense, the truth or reality of life.

conditioned self (see also *personal self*): What in Western psychology might be termed ego, it is those aspects of self that are limited by circumstance, body, individuality.

daishin: See *magnanimous mind*.

dharma: (1) things, phenomena; (2) the object of our thoughts; (3) the Buddha's teaching; (4) Law, truth.

dharma world (Skt., *dharmadhatu*): The entire universe inclusive of all things.

Dōgen (1200–1253): Founder of Soto Zen in Japan. He is referred to as Dōgen or Dōgen Zenji (an honorific term; see *zenji*) and, more formally, as Eihei Dōgen or Eihei Dōgen Zenji. Dōgen wrote voluminously on the interpretation of Buddhism and Zen, as well as on Buddhist practice. His more philosophical writings are included in his ninety-five-chapter *Shōbōgenzō*. His writings on practice include the *Eihei Shingi (Regulations for Eihei Monastery), Zuimonki (Dōgen's Informal Talks),* and *Gakudō Yōjinsū (Points to Consider in Studying and Practicing The Way).*

faith: The process of clarifying and becoming lucid about the structure and workings of the life force.

hinayana: Originally, a pejorative term applied to Buddhists who seek salvation only for themselves. Dōgen used the term to suggest a narrow attitude in regard to practice.

impermanence (Jp., *shogyō mujō*): The doctrine that all things are changing, passing, unfixed.

interdependence (Jp., *engi;* Skt., *pratitya-samutpada*): The doctrine that all things are dependent on every other thing.

jijuyu zanmai: The total immersion of one's life whereby everything encountered is encountered totally and not half-heartedly.

jinissai jiko: A term coined by Dōgen to indicate an all-inclusive definition of self, referred to in this book as "universal self."

joyful mind (Jp., *kishin*): Having a deep sense of joy and thankfulness that one is able to carry out whatever task is at hand.

kakusoku: Literally, "wake up and touch." It means to wake up to and have intimate contact with true reality—and to actually live out that reality. It is very similar in meaning to *jijuyū zanmai.*

karma: One's actions, often connected with causal relationships.

kenshō: To see into or realize one's true nature.

kinhin: Walking Zen, often practiced between periods of zazen.

kishin: See *joyful mind.*

Kōdō Sawaki Roshi: See *Sawaki Roshi.*

kyōsaku: A wooden stick used to wake up the zazen sitter who has fallen asleep.

magnanimous mind (Jp., *daishin*): The mind or attitude of viewing a situation or one's life from as broad a perspective as possible.

Mahayana Buddhism (Jp., *Daijō Bukkyō*): One of the two major branches of Buddhism; includes Zen, Pure Land, and many other schools. The central teaching is that any practice is never for oneself alone, but for all people.

Middle Way (Jp., *chūdō*): The Buddha's teaching, also expounded by Nagarjuna, that reality lies beyond all sensual or intellectual dualities of pain and pleasure, or of right and wrong.

mumyō (Skt., *avidya*): Darkness or ignorance.

nehan jakujō: Literally "nirvana is tranquillity"; one of the three signs of the Buddha's teachings, intended to draw ordinary people away from the illusion of life and death and toward nirvana, or peace beyond all understanding.

nembutsu: Recitation of Amida Buddha's name—that is, to say "Namu amida butsu," which means "Homage to Amida Buddha."

nurturing mind (Jp., *rōshin*): This is the nurturing attitude of a parent toward her or his child, but in a broader sense, a person's attitude toward everything she or he encounters in life. The original term was *rōba shinsetsu,* literally, the kindness of a grandmother.

opening the hand of thought (Jp., *omoi no te banashi*): Uchiyama Roshi's expression that graphically describes the mental posture during zazen.

original self (Jp., *honrai no jiko*): The original state of things prior to processing, discriminating, analyzing, and organizing them by thought.

parental mind: See *nurturing mind.*

patriarch: See *ancestors.*

personal self: Who each of us is as a collection of our past and present circumstances, our wishes and ideas, and the identities of which we clothe ourselves.

pratyekabuddha: (Jp., *engaku,* also *byakushibutsu* or *dokkaku*): One of two kinds of hinayana sages, one who attains liberation without a teacher's guidance.

Pure Land Buddhism: The Buddhist teaching propagated in Japan by Hōnen and Shinran that all people are saved by Amida Buddha and will eventually go to the Western Paradise, or Pure Land.

reality: In Buddhist terminology, *shinnyo,* the ultimate reality.

reality of life (Jp., *seimei no jitsubutsu*): An early expression of Uchiyama Roshi meaning true reality or, in Buddhist terminology, *shinnyo.* "The activity of the reality of life" is a translation of *seimei no jitsubutsu no hataraki*—that is, the work or function of the life force.

repentance: The attitude or posture of a repentant Zen practitioner, not merely to feel sorry or remorseful but to sit zazen. Zazen is the ultimate posture of repentance.

roshi (Jp., *rōshi*): In Zen, a highly respected teacher. It is used at the end of a name, as in Uchiyama Roshi and Sawaki Roshi.

rōshin: See *nurturing mind*.

samadhi (Jp., *zanmai*): In a narrow sense, a focusing of one's concentration on one object, but in a much broader sense, being concentrated and pouring all one's energies into each activity.

sanbōin: Literally, the three seals of the Buddhist law or teaching. They are *shogyō mujō,* all things are impermanent; *shohō muga,* there is no unchanging, substantial self; and *nehan jakujō,* peace beyond desire. See *shihōin.*

sangai kaiku: Suffering, the second undeniable reality. See *shihōin.*

sangha (Jp., *sōrin*): The gathering of three or more people to practice Buddhism.

satori: Realization or enlightenment.

Sawaki Roshi: Former abbot of Antaiji, he died in 1965, at which time his senior disciple, Kōshō Uchiyama Roshi, became abbot. Kōdō Sawaki Roshi spent only a few days each month at Antaiji during his tenure as abbot because he traveled around the country continually, conducting sesshins and giving dharma lectures on Zen.

self (Jp., *jiko*): Used here generally to refer to the whole, inclusive, original, or universal self that includes the personal, conditioned, individual self.

self making the self out of the self, self doing itself by itself (Jp., *jiko ga jiko o jiko suru*): An enigmatic expression of Sawaki Roshi's, indicating that the subject, object, and function of self is *jiko,* or self.

self that is only self (Jp., *jiko giri no jiko*): Coined by Uchiyama Roshi to urge followers not to speculate about what self might be. The expression is meant to indicate that there is nothing outside of self. It should be understood in a nondualistic way, and has no connection to ego-centricity or self-centeredness.

sesshin: Long periods of zazen, sometimes extending for several days or weeks.

Shakyamuni Buddha: The historical figure who attained complete enlightenment under the bodhi tree; the founder of Buddhism.

shihōin: The four seals of the Buddhist teaching. They are the three seals, or *sanbōin,* plus *sangai kaiku,* the second undeniable reality, that all beings suffer. See also *sanbōin.*

shikantaza: Eihei Dōgen Zenji's expression for zazen. Literally, *shikantaza* means "just sitting," or "only sitting." For a fuller discussion see *Soto Zen—An Introduction to Zazen,* edited by and available from the Soto Zen International Center in San Francisco (info@sotozen.com).

Shōbōgenzō: The major philosophical explanation of Buddhism by Eihei Dōgen Zenji, containing ninety-five chapters.

shogyō mujō: See *impermanence, sanbōin.*

shohō jissō: All things are ultimate reality as they are. The expression appears in the Lotus Sutra.

shohō muga: All things are without a permanent, fixed, substantial self. See also sanbōin.

shōjō no shu: Practice based on enlightenment.

shravaka: Originally, a disciple of the Buddha; later, a follower who contemplates the principle of the fourfold noble truth to attain nirvana.

shushō ichinyo: The identity of practice and enlightenment.

tanden: An area a few inches below the navel and around the abdomen.

tathata: Suchness, thusness.

three minds (of Dōgen): See *magnanimous mind, nurturing mind,* and *joyful mind.*

three seals: See *sanbōin.*

universal life, universal self: Refers to the inclusive and endless aspect of life and the shared nature of the life force of all beings.

vow: Life direction.

Way, Buddha Way: To seek or follow the Buddha Way means to focus all your effort on the most genuine way to live, and to continually refine your life.

zabuton: Large square cushion on which a smaller round cushion called a *zafu* is placed during zazen.

zafu: Round cushion used to sit on during zazen.

zazen: In the narrow sense, the term is used to indicate a particular sitting posture, though Uchiyama Roshi uses the expression "a life of zazen" to point out a way of life centered on a sitting practice. The attitude with which one sits subsequently affects one's attitude during all one's actions. The word should not be confused with the English word "meditation," even though many Zen Buddhists use the word synonymously with it, simply because the English word already carries its own connotations.

zendo: A hall used just for sitting in zazen, or a place dedicated to zazen.

zenji: An old Buddhist term that originally referred to any Zen practitioner, but in later periods came to be used exclusively in the Zen schools as an honorific title meaning "Zen teacher or master." In the Soto Zen tradition only the abbots of the two head monasteries, Eiheiji and Sōjiji, are called *zenji*. It is used after the name, as in Dōgen Zenji and Keizan Zenji.

Index

About the Author
and Translators

Kōshō Uchiyama was born in Tokyo in 1912. He received
a master's degree in Western philosophy at Waseda
University in 1937 and became a Zen priest three years
later under Kōdō Sawaki Roshi. Upon Sawaki's death in
1965, he became abbot of Antaiji, a temple and monastery then located on the outskirts of Kyoto. Uchiyama
Roshi developed the practice at Antaiji and occasionally
traveled in Japan, lecturing and leading sesshins. The
three pillars of his practice were his writings, his time
spent guiding and talking with disciples and visitors,
and zazen, the sitting practice itself. He retired from
Antaiji in 1975 and lived with his wife at Noke-in, a
small temple outside Kyoto, where he continued to
write, publish, and meet with the many people who
found their way to his door, until his death in 1998. He
wrote over twenty books on Zen, including translations
of Dōgen Zenji in modern Japanese with commentaries,
a few of which are available in English, as are various

shorter essays. He was an origami master as well as a Zen master and published several books on origami.

Daitsu Tom Wright was born and raised in Watertown, Wisconsin, and lived in Japan for over forty years. He practiced and studied Zen under Uchiyama Roshi from 1968 until the latter's death. He was ordained as a priest by Uchiyama Roshi in 1974. A graduate of the University of Wisconsin in Oriental Languages and Literature, he received a master's in humanities and English literature at California State University. He is currently emeritus professor at Ryukoku University in Kyoto, Japan, where he taught in the English language and culture program. He was a teacher for the Kyoto Soto Zen Center until 1995, and later led zazen gatherings with Doyu Takamine Roshi at Seitaian Temple in Kyoto and Senkokuji Temple in Tamba, until 2010. Rev. Wright has worked on the translation and editing of several texts of Dōgen Zenji, along with the commentaries of Uchiyama Roshi. He was the co-translator, with Steve Yenik, of an early version of this book in 1973, *Approach to Zen*, and of the first edition of *Opening the Hand of Thought* in 1993, as well as a co-translator, with Shohaku Okumura, of *Deepest Practice, Deepest Wisdom: Three Fascicles from Shōbōgenzō with Commentary* by Kōshō Uchiyama. Rev. Wright continues to work on more translations of Dōgen Zenji's works, accompanied by commentaries by Uchiyama Roshi and his own understanding of the texts. He is married and has one son, and currently lives in Hawai'i with his wife, Yuko. He also teaches at Alaneo Zendo (abbot, Myoshin Kaniumoe) in Hilo.

Jisho Warner is a Soto Zen priest and teacher. She grew up in New York City and graduated from Harvard University in 1965. A disciple of Rev. Tozen Akiyama, she did monastic training in the United States under Dainin Katagiri Roshi at Hokyoji in Minnesota, and in Japan under Shundo Aoyama Roshi at Aichi Senmon Nisodo in Nagoya. An artist before becoming a Zen priest, Reverend Warner was also an editor for many years and was instrumental in the first edition of *Opening the Hand of Thought* as well as many other books on the Buddhist dharma. She first encountered the teachings of Uchiyama Roshi in the early 1980s, when she practiced at Pioneer Valley Zendo in Massachusetts under a disciple of Uchiyama Roshi's, Reverend Koshi Ichida. Rev. Warner is the founding teacher at Stone Creek Zendo in Sebastopol, California, where she currently leads practice.

Shohaku Okumura is a Soto Zen priest and Dharma successor of Kōshō Uchiyama Roshi. He is a graduate of Komazawa University and has practiced in Japan at Antaiji, Zuioji, and the Kyoto Soto Zen Center, and in Massachusetts at the Pioneer Valley Zendo. He is the former director of the Soto Zen Buddhism International Center in San Francisco. Besides Uchiyama Roshi's *Opening the Hand of Thought* and *Deepest Practice, Deepest Wisdom*, he is the co-translator, with Taigen Dan Leighton, of *Dogen's Extensive Record: A Translation of the Eihei Koroku*, and the translator and co-author, with Kōshō Uchiyama, of *The Zen Teaching of Homeless Kodo*. He is the author of *Living by Vow: A Practical Introduction to Eight Essential Zen Chants and Texts*, *The Mountains and Waters Sutra: A Practitioner's Guide to Dōgen's "Sansuikyo,"* and *Realizing Genjōkoan: The Key to Dogen's Shobogenzo*. He is the founding teacher of the Sanshin Zen Community, based in Bloomington, Indiana, where he lives with his family.

Acknowledgments

We would like to thank all the many people who have read and commented to us on *Opening the Hand of Thought;* we have tried to incorporate those suggestions. A number of people gave hands-on help, some of it extensive. Steve Yenik was instrumental in creating *Approach to Zen,* which became part of *Opening the Hand of Thought.* Fred Stoeber worked very hard on the parts of *Opening the Hand* that talk about modern civilization and Zen. Josh Bartok at Wisdom Publications provided considerable help. Tai Hazard drew wonderful illustrations, with life and breath in them, and Marilyn Chuck skillfully refined and digitized them. Irene Flynn created the fine index with great care. Joan Goldsmith and Yūkō Wright were supportive at every turn. We are grateful to them all. Our deep appreciation goes to everyone who engages in this marvelous practice.

What to Read Next
from Wisdom Publications

The Zen Teaching of Homeless Kodo
Kosho Uchiyama and Shohaku Okumura

Deepest Practice, Deepest Wisdom
Three Fascicles from Shobogenzo with Commentary
Kosho Uchiyama
Translated by Daitsu Tom Wright and Shohaku Okumura

Dogen's Extensive Record
A Translation of the Eihei Koroku
Translated by Taigen Dan Leighton and Shohaku Okumura

Living by Vow
A Practical Introduction to Eight Essential Zen Chants and Texts
Shohaku Okumura

The Mountains and Waters Sutra
A Practitioner's Guide to Dōgen's "Sansuikyo"
Shohaku Okumura

Realizing Genjōkoan
The Key to Dogen's Shobogenzo.
Shohaku Okumura

On Zen Practice
Body, Breath, and Mind
Edited by Taizan Maezumi Roshi and Bernie Glassman
Foreword by Robert Aitken

Novice to Master
An Ongoing Lesson in the Extent of My Own Stupidity
by Soko Morinaga Roshi
Translated by Belenda Attaway Yamakawa

Faces of Compassion
Classic Bodhisattva Archetypes and
Their Modern Expression
Taigen Dan Leighton
Foreword by Joan Halifax

Trust in Mind
The Rebellion of Chinese Zen
Mu Soeng
Foreword by Jan Chozen Bays

About Wisdom Publications

Wisdom Publications is the leading publisher of classic and contemporary Buddhist books and practical works on mindfulness. To learn more about us or to explore our other books, please visit our website at wisdomexperience .org or contact us at the address below.

Wisdom Publications
199 Elm Street
Somerville, MA 02144 USA

We are a 501(c)(3) organization, and donations in support of our mission are tax deductible.

Wisdom Publications is affiliated with the Foundation for the Preservation of the Mahayana Tradition (FPMT).